OTHER TITLES BY ROLAND S. BARTH

Improving Schools from Within

Cruising Rules

Run School Run

Open Education and the American School

LEARNING BY HEART

LEARNING BY HEART

Roland S. Barth

Foreword by

Deborah Meier

JOSSEY-BASS
A Wiley Company
www.josseybass.com

Published by

www.josseybass.com

Credits appear on page 246.

Library of Congress Cataloging-in-Publication Data

Barth, Roland S.
Learning by heart / Roland S. Barth; foreword by Deborah Meier.—1st ed.
p. cm.—(The Jossey-Bass education series)
Includes bibliographical references and index.
ISBN 0-7879-5543-4
1. Education—Aims and objectives—United States. 2. Educational change—United States. 3. Effective teaching—United States. 4. Group work in education—United States. 5. Learning. I. Title. II. Series.
LA217.2.B397 2001
371.102—dc21

00-012938

FIRST EDITION
HB Printing 10 9 8 7 6 5 4

The Jossey-Bass Education Series

To Barbara

the breeze in my sails

CONTENTS

FOREWORD

In *Learning by Heart*, Roland Barth offers educators a refreshingly vibrant and clear voice in the midst of the current turbulent debate about school reform and the future of education. Most of us signed up for this profession because we want to use our hearts as well as our minds in order to promote young people's learning; because we believe deeply that learning is one of the noblest, most profound endeavors of the human experience; and because we are firmly committed to the value of learning in a democratic community. *Learning by Heart* speaks to us. From these pages emerges a strong sense of pride in those feelings, values, and beliefs, as well as a call to action that is challenging, compelling—and irresistible.

Barth knows that the current "top down" approach to education—the imposed external standards, the high-stakes tests, the legislative mandates—are all neglecting the heart and killing the soul of the profession and demeaning the richness of the experience and insights of those who have devoted themselves to it. Consequently, he sets out to have conversations with those of us in the schoolhouse: the teachers, students, parents, and principals who make up the community of a school.

Barth is preaching in this book, and like any good preacher he tells good stories, recalls old wisdoms, and, perhaps most important, draws from a long personal history of having been there. I'm one of those many people whose work has depended on Barth's capacity to clear the underbrush and let us see where next to set our feet.

The strength of this book comes from its lucid vision of what a school hospitable to human learning looks like, and from its equally detailed description, through many examples, of good education in practice. It's one thing to write about how the world of education should look; how a community of learners and leaders should be attained; how teachers, principals, and administrators should collaborate and share leadership. But of even greater interest to most practitioners is how to make these things happen. From his years of being in the field, working on the front lines with other educators, Roland Barth brings to the table the experiences and the practical wisdom—the craft knowledge—gleaned from success and failure, and shares the riches with us. Although it is certainly idealistic, this book is also practical about what it is we know about school renewal and the kind of support systems that must be developed to initiate and sustain such renewal.

Ever the realist, Barth doesn't ignore or dismiss the impediments facing the profession in its long, hard struggle for recognition and improvement. In fact, he offers us a generous dose of skepticism, and reminds us that there are as many reasons, some of them quite valid, to think that schools cannot "fix themselves" as there are to think they can. Rather than insult us with the usual overdoses of cheerleading, slogans, and "just try a little harder" advice, he invites us to confront and tackle together with him the many formidable challenges to improving our schools. He knows that no one can scale these heights alone.

Barth is an unredeemed democrat. The kind of intellectual life he thrives on himself and is banking on for the rest of us is one that is built on thinking for oneself. To be in his presence, and to read his work, are constant reminders of his democratic underpinnings. Yet he knows that thinking for oneself is a highly social activity. It requires community. It requires other people to push back as you reason your way to a better truth. And it requires a very strong community to argue respectfully with folks you think are just plumb wrong.

I once had a conversation with Roland during which I told him that I had discovered too late in life that my dream of being a pilot was based on a mistaken view: what I really wanted was to be a bird. "There's hang-gliding," he reminded me. Don't give up on the dream; if we really know what it is we want, we can find ways to get there. So, yes, I'm considering hang-gliding. My heart is willing. But learning by heart also requires a good friend and mentor to see one through, one who helps you keep your dreams alive. Roland Barth is that friend and mentor.

Barth challenges us so that we will challenge ourselves—and rise to the occasion. He values us so that we will value ourselves—and translate our values into actions. And he believes in us so that we will believe in ourselves—and find the strength and courage we need not only to stay this difficult, stormy course of education reform but also to give our hearts to it, and to thrive in it.

Deborah Meier
Principal
Mission Hill Elementary School
Boston

ACKNOWLEDGMENTS

I want to thank the many educators throughout the world whose schools I have visited and with whom I have had conversations over the years. The rich insights, generously shared, of teachers, principals, central office administrators, and parents have been the primary knowledge base upon which I have relied in writing *Learning by Heart*.

I would also like to thank the many readers who have withstood early drafts of the manuscript. In particular, the heroic efforts and helpful comments of Jay Casbon, Gordon Donaldson, Phil Hunsberger, Kathy Asheton-Miller, Gayle Moller, and Joe Richardson have helped transform my words—which sometimes resemble a sow's ear—into much better words—which sometimes resemble a silk purse. And my deep appreciation to my sister, Vanessa, who one again succeeded in processing and typing my words through six drafts.

And I want to acknowledge with admiration the exhaustive and exhausting efforts by the editors at Jossey-Bass. In particular, senior editor Lesley Iura and copyeditor Michele Jones helped further rearrange these words into more coherent prose.

Finally, I want to thank my wife, Barbara Bauman, for her patience, acumen, and endless conversations with me spent "wordfarming" in Maine and on trains, boats, planes, and assorted other places. Together, we may have elevated these words and this prose into what even might be called literature.

Head Tide, Maine R. S. B.
December 2000

THE AUTHOR

Roland S. Barth is a consultant to schools, school systems, state departments of education, universities, foundations, and businesses in the United States and abroad.

After receiving his A.B. degree in psychology from Princeton University and master's and doctoral degrees in education from Harvard University, he served as a public school teacher and principal for fifteen years in Massachusetts, Connecticut, and California.

Barth was the recipient of a Guggenheim Fellowship. He was a member of the faculty at the Harvard Graduate School of Education for thirteen years. During that time, he was senior lecturer and director of the Study on the Harvard Graduate School of Education and Schools, as well as founding director of the Principals' Center and of the International Network of Principals' Centers. He has been an academic visitor at Oxford University and a member of the National Commission on Excellence in Educational Administration.

Barth is also the recipient of an honorary Doctor of Humane Letters from Lewis and Clark College, a trustee of Hurricane Island Outward Bound School, a member of the board of MicroSociety Inc. and chairman of the board of the Aspiring Principals' Program. He currently serves on the board of editorial advisers of the *Phi Delta Kappan*.

Barth is author of many articles and of four books: *Cruising Rules* (1998), *Improving Schools from Within* (1990), *Run School Run* (1980), and *Open Education and the American School* (1972).

His particular fields of interest are school leadership, school improvement from within, and the personal and professional development of educators. Central to his thinking are the concepts of the school as a community of learners and the school as a community of leaders.

Roland Barth is the father of two accomplished daughters, Joanna and Carolyn, an avid sailor of Maine and Florida salt waters, and a dedicated farmer. He and his wife Barbara divide their time among Maine, Florida, and Boston.

INTRODUCTION

> What is done is done for the love of it—or not really done at all. —*Robert Frost*

Tidying up her home as she was preparing to move to another kind of home, my mother recently presented me a tattered, treasured box full of my school report cards. A most interesting literature. One comment (which accompanied a grade of C–) jumped out; my insightful junior high social studies teacher observed back in 1949, rather poetically, that "Roland did some things well—and just did some things." This same appraisal, a half-century later, might be offered of our profession. We're doing some things well—and just doing some other things.

Ten years ago I completed a little book, *Improving Schools from Within*, in which I reflected on the state of things in schools and made several suggestions for improvement. Well, public schools have, by most standards, improved in many ways in the past decade. SAT scores and attendance rates are generally up; discipline problems and dropout rates are generally down. High school students are taking tougher courses, and more are going to college. But these improvements have been attained at considerable cost: schools are taking a disturbing toll on the teachers and administrators who labor within them.

I have a bad back. My good orthopedic surgeon discouraged me from going under the knife. His reasoning: many bad backs are a consequence not of structural failures but of emotional overloading, especially anger. As in "that gets my back up." My wise physician further reasoned that certain professions generate more anger than others. Teachers and administrators, he reported, seem to work with one or both hands tied behind them while they are battered by all sorts of blows from imperious central office staff, disrespectful parents, and troublesome students. And they can't fight back. Hence endemic anger and a predisposition to back problems within the education profession.

Despite exercises, acupuncture, and pills, my back pain persisted. In search of relief I underwent surgery, whereupon I encountered something with which few school people have ever had to contend: discretionary time. About a month of it. For a week or so I lay on my back, watching videos, taking pills, and feeling sorry for myself. Then a voice—that persistent New England Calvinist voice, so familiar to educators—began to intrude: "Roland, you really ought to be doing something *useful* with this time."

I listened, and responded by asking a friend to bring home from my office the sedimentary deposits of reading materials I had been carefully collecting at the back of my desk. National studies, state reports, *Phi Delta Kappans*, books, and book manuscripts had been accumulating for many years with the promise, "When I get time, I want to read this." Now was the moment of truth. I was either going to read this stuff or throw it away and no longer delude myself. So I began to read conscientiously through the literature of school reform since about 1983 and the seminal federal report *A Nation at Risk*. I soon encountered the household names so familiar in our profession: Ted Sizer, James Comer, John Goodlad, Mortimer Adler, and Ron Edmonds, among others.

I kept reading. After a couple of weeks of this treatment, my back began to hurt again. I kept reading. It hurt more. One morning I came in touch with what many members of the male species have now come to call a "feeling." I was pleased that I could detect that I was having one and even prouder that I could name and express the feeling: *anger!* Again. So why, I asked myself, were the good works of these good people—all well-intentioned, capable reformers of America's schools—making me so angry? It dawned on me that behind the models, the rubrics, the principles, the analyses of the problems, and the prescriptions for improving them was a very chilling assumption: *schools are not capable of improving them-*

selves. Those who labor each day under the roof of the schoolhouse—teachers, principals, librarians, secretaries, social workers, psychologists, custodians, special education instructors, and, not least, students—are not capable of getting their own house in order. Else, why do you need these outside interventions?

Allow me to share a few gleanings from my recuperative reading exercise.

From government: in recent years, all fifty states have passed sweeping legislation mandating that by next June every school will have improved. Common to most of these bills—for example, Colorado's 1337, Texas's H.B. 72, Michigan's Public Act 25, and Washington's H.B. 1209—are requirements like these:

> Each school shall have a vision or mission statement that indicates the direction in which the school wants to head.
>
> Each school shall have a strategic plan showing precisely the means to be employed and along what timeline.
>
> Each school shall have a school improvement council or school improvement team, which will be responsible for leading this effort.
>
> Each school shall conduct an annual audit and disclose the following to the public and higher officials: attendance rates, dropout rates, discipline rates, scores from standardized tests, teacher turnover rates, and other such information.

Behind the thinking of the legislatures in Denver, Austin, Lansing, and Olympia, of course, is the assumption that unless they pass these laws, schools in the state will be the same next September as last. Indeed, years after *A Nation at Risk*, the Education Commission of the States estimated that fewer than 4 percent of our nation's schools have made any significant effort to restructure.

Schools are not capable of improving themselves.

From business: businesses are weighing in very heavily these days with concern about the quality of new employees coming out of the schools. The *poor* quality. They report spending annually an estimated $25 billion teaching new hires what they need to know but didn't learn in school: writing, reading, reasoning, problem solving, teamwork. Businesses are not happy about this. Many are taking constructive steps to help. The World Class Schools project of the Florida Chamber of Commerce is one example of such efforts. Chris Whittle's Edison Schools are another.

But less charitable voices abound. I remember reading in a dentist's office a business magazine in which the lead article was about the deplorable conditions in America's schools. I forgot—or repressed—most of the story, but I vividly recall the conclusion, the essence of which was something like this: To survive, America's public schools must be totally restructured, top to bottom—all of them—and they will never reform themselves. Only a powerful outside presence will lead to that.

Schools are not capable of improving themselves.

From academia: many colleges and universities have crafted helpful, equitable partnerships with the public schools. New York University's Professional Development Laboratory is a good case in point, as are many principals' centers hosted by universities. But I'm afraid few academics entertain much hope that substantive school improvement will ever come from within.

Professor Robert E. Slavin of Johns Hopkins University is the founder of Success For All, a popular program for raising achievement levels of elementary school students. Slavin argues that "only a handful of schools—perhaps less than 5 percent of elementary or secondary schools in the entire country—have the capacity to translate reform, guided by general principles, into reality."[1]

Another academic put it even less charitably: "Attempts by schools to improve themselves consist of a basic pattern of grand pretensions, faulty execution and puny results."

Schools are not capable of improving themselves! To paraphrase one of Sir Isaac Newton's Laws of Motion, a school at rest will remain at rest until acted upon by an outside force.

So there you have it, votes of no confidence emanating from the worlds of government, business, and academia. Many in the central office would no doubt concur. All convey the same chilling message: schools are not capable of improving themselves. Or, put more crudely, "You guys are losers."

It's a curious situation. Those outside of schools have precious little confidence that those inside of schools can improve much. Yet when I invite teachers and principals to "stand up if you believe that *your* school is capable of major, systemic reform—pretty much on its own"—most stand. And when I talk with teachers and principals and others inside schools, they are quick to report little confidence that those outside of schools can really do much to change their schools—whether it be by passing a law, "adopting" a school, or generating a theoretical model. Or I should say that these educators believe that those outside schools can do quite a lot to change schools but very little to *improve* them.

All of this raises a troublesome, discouraging question: If schools can't be improved from within or from without, just how will they ever be transformed into places of profound learning for youngsters in the twenty-first century?

I must admit that, as a principal, I had fantasies of transporting my public school way up to the Northeast Kingdom of Vermont where there would be no central office, no state department, no parents. Then, I reasoned, we could blow the kids' socks off and create a wonderful school. But of course, schools then, as now, are not islands. Few can really invigorate themselves without outside resources. All need ideas, funds, buses, books, curricula, and a support system, and all need parents in their cheering section. The school-based reformer cannot work alone within the school any better than the teacher can work alone behind a closed classroom door.

The question isn't whether a school can improve with or without these outside resources; the question is whether the school will be (as we say in academia) the dependent variable, the independent variable, or the interdependent variable in its relationship with the outside world. All too many people both inside and outside of schools have settled on the school as the dependent variable, responding to the wishes and whims of the outside world.

There are dangers in assuming that the other guy is always the dependent variable. A sailing friend recently sent me an e-mail of the following illustrative anecdote, reportedly a transmission of a U.S. Navy radio conversation:

> *Transmission:* Please divert your course fifteen degrees north to avoid a collision.
>
> *Response:* Recommend that you divert your course fifteen degrees south to avoid a collision.
>
> *Transmission:* This is the captain of a U.S. Naval ship. I say again, divert your course.
>
> *Response:* No, I say again, divert *your* course.
>
> *Transmission: This is the aircraft carrier* Enterprise. *We are a large warship of the U.S. Navy. Divert your course now!*
>
> *Response:* This is a lighthouse. Your call.

I believe that schools are lighthouses. I believe that every school harbors within its walls the capacity for grown-ups and students to become inventors and reformers, to engage in authentic change. I have worked in schools as a teacher, vice principal, and principal; I have worked in and around schools with state departments of education, principals' centers, universities, and businesses. My experience leads me to believe that schools and the teachers, parents, administrators, and students who inhabit them are *quite* capable of improving their places. If the conditions are right, if certain planets can be brought into alignment, I believe it becomes not only possible but likely that a school, any school, can become a continually self-renewing enterprise. The school that becomes a self-renewing enterprise will shape its own future. The constructive leader for such a school identifies and then introduces these conditions into the culture of the school.

Most of us—teachers, principals, and other school people—signed up for this profession because we care deeply about our important place in the lives of students. To put it simply: in addition to a brain, we have a heart—and we want to put it to use in promoting young people's learning. Exclude this vital organ from our work, and you get compliance at best. Obedience may make superordinates feel influential, but it won't go very far toward making school educators feel influential, and won't, therefore, go very far toward improving our schools.

My intent in this book is not academic explication, which is readily abundant elsewhere in our profession. Rather, I want to engage you, the reader, in something like the conversations we've all had in the teachers' lounge—conversations about how to make our schools work better. Indeed, most of what I have to say here is based on conversations about school reform, observations, and experiences I've had with teachers, principals, and other school-based educators over the past decade.

That great Eastern philosopher Yogi Berra was reportedly once told by his seventh-grade teacher, "Yogi, you don't know *anything!*" Whereupon Yogi is said to have replied in his unmistakable diction, "Not only don't I not know anything, I don't even *suspect* anything." I'm not sure what I know about improving schools, but I do suspect some things. The purpose of this little volume is to offer what I suspect are the most important conditions in a school's culture that support the renewal of the school and of all who live and labor there. Only when those conditions exist will the schoolhouse become a place hospitable to profound learning by young and old alike.

And I want to make my back feel better!

Head Tide, Maine
December 2000

Roland S. Barth

I

THINKING OTHERWISE

> To achieve excellence one must want to become good enough bad enough.
>
> —*Pete Carrill, former basketball coach, Princeton University*

Reform has become both a source of hope and a platitude in our profession. It is a big tent under which many people are doing and saying many things. It is a concept that means different things to different people and may, therefore, be in danger of becoming altogether meaningless. At the same time, reform has become a watchword for all of us who care deeply about good schools. I find the turn of the century to be a remarkable window of opportunity for educators. For me, it is the most exciting moment in forty years in this profession.

When I was teaching fifth grade, and then as a school principal, I used to hear a statement in the teachers' lounge that infuriated me. We've all heard of four-letter words. This was a four-word sentence, predictably uttered every time any of us came up with a new idea: "They'll never let us." Maybe Albert Einstein was right when he said, "Great ideas have always encountered violent opposition from mediocre minds"!

"They'll never let us" was a wet blanket against which we fought in the struggle to maintain our enthusiasm. I never knew who "they" were, nor did I ever care to find out. However, I did discover that if I could identify a practice I thought was in the best interest of students, if I had a pretty clear rationale for it, and if against all odds I could enlist the support of some teachers, parents, and administrators, we could usually act on the idea, and "they" would not jump out from behind a bush and kill it. We were able to achieve one of my biggest objectives for the school—what diplomats in Washington call diplomatic immunity. In short, we could determine our own future.

The expression *improving schools from within* has at least two meanings: first, those who work under the roof of the schoolhouse must do it; second, school people must confront the cautious, resistant, fearful "other" that resides within each of us before confronting the others who are without. Those others may be fewer and less intimidating than we imagine. Pogo, the little opossum in Walt Kelly's comic strip, had it right: We have met the enemy and he is us.

Things in schools have changed dramatically over the past few years. Now "they" not only permit us to proceed with a new idea, they expect and demand that we do. As one principal recently put it: "If I had shared my vision of a school ten years ago, I would have been locked up. Now, I can't get a job without a vision."

Lick the Envelope

I heard recently a wonderful definition for *professor* that comes from medieval German universities: one who thinks otherwise. In this era of reform, school people are invited to be professors—to think otherwise. Thinking otherwise does not necessarily mean thinking big rather than small about good education. It means thinking differently. Let's say you don't like the taste you get when you lick postage stamps. You could think big and try to get the U.S. government to use mint flavoring. Or you could endure years of revulsion or curtail your correspondence. Or you could do what one teacher did—lick the envelope rather than the stamp. *That* is a "paradigm shift"!

I visited Alaska recently. There I found several folks thinking otherwise. In Juneau, a city where rain is more plentiful than sunshine, schools are occasionally shut down, not for "snow days" or "rain days," but for "sun days." In Fairbanks I found another school thinking otherwise. Instead of engaging in the demeaning practice of being adopted by a business, this school adopted a shopping center. There were about as many shops in the center as classrooms in the school, so each class adopted a shop. Fourth graders cleaned the cages of turtles and hamsters in the pet store. Other students rearranged displays in the five-and-dime. The shopping center, as you might expect, took a sudden interest in the school. The stationery store designed and printed a new school letterhead. The drapery shop spruced up the teachers' lounge. Think otherwise.

Yet another school discovered that many students are more comfortable with and know far more about computers than do most adults. In this school, these students are now called "teachers." They give regular instruction in word processing, programming, and the Internet to many other "students"—including teachers, parents, and administrators. The school is becoming a community in which everyone, children and adults alike, engages visibly and simultaneously in its most important enterprise. Think otherwise.

Sheep and Goats

I recall hearing another common response from children when I was a teacher and from teachers when I was a principal. I found it as troublesome as the defeatist four-word sentence. This one was a question: "What am I supposed to do?"

There are a number of things that schools don't teach very well. One thing they do seem to teach with remarkable success is dependency. A bill is passed by the state legislature mandating, say, drug education. It is sent to the state department of education to be implemented. Those in the department look it over and ask, "What are we supposed to do?" Then they tool up some language and send memos to the school superintendents in the state. A superintendent looks it over and asks, "What am I supposed to do?" Then the superintendent sends it along to principals, who in turn ask, "What am I supposed to do?" The principal writes up a memo and puts it into teachers' boxes. A teacher, rushing from recess duty to class, looks it over and asks, "What am I supposed to do?" Shortly thereafter, materials appear on students' desks. In turn each student asks, "What am I supposed to do?" And so it goes.

For some reason, occupants of schools seem destined to comply. What I do is in response to what someone else tells me to do. Or, as one principal put it, "Most of what teachers teach is of no real interest to them; it is only what teachers think someone wants students to know."

Education is a very loosely coupled enterprise, but we never seem to tire of trying to tightly couple it. We never quite shake the illusion that if you issue a mandate in one place at one level, it will be faithfully carried out in another place at another level. In reality, of course, what students in classes of compliant teachers are doing by way of drug education bears little resemblance to what legislators had in mind when they passed the bill.

Teachers and principals are gifted and talented at resisting even the good ideas inflicted upon them from above—whether "above" means Washington, the state department of education, or the central office. It should be intuitively obvious that no one can change a school very much without the cooperation of the teachers and administrators. Regrettably, many have yet to learn this.

The illusion of tight coupling depends for its success on the existence of bright sheep—that is, on the presence of very capable individuals who, with eagerness and inventiveness, will invest great energy in faithfully complying with the directives of others. Sheep, of course, don't come that way. We can have bright, willful, ornery goats—or dumb, obedient, docile, plodding sheep. I'm afraid our profession is repelling many of the goats, who, though they have a stomach for tin cans, have little appetite for mindless compliance with the heavy-handed "tougher" standards. And we're attracting many sheep who can and will comply, but with little distinction.

Bright goats who stay are finding it necessary in their work as educators to maintain two sets of books. One set consists of the things these teachers must do that give the illusion of compliance and will ensure they do not get fired: fifteen minutes a week of drug instruction, drilling students in preparation for the standardized tests, and so on.

The second set of books consists of those matters educators passionately believe in. *This* is why they entered the profession. These are the things they do that enable them to maintain their self-respect, integrity, passion, and heart: relating a recent summer spent in Italy to a unit on the Renaissance, assisting a student who wants to devise an unusual science experiment. Unfortunately, these days few teachers experience much congruence between the two sets of books.

Our profession desperately needs school-based reformers. A school-based reformer is an educator who works in the school and is seldom heard to say, "They'll never let us," and seldom asks, "What am I supposed to do?" A school-based reformer is frequently a goat who thinks otherwise, one who works very hard to maintain *one* set of books by asking, What is it that I believe constitutes a good education for these youngsters? and How am I going to enlist resources to change this school so that we can provide that education?

When I was an elementary school teacher and a principal, my colleagues and I experienced our work as a profession, even a calling. At the turn of the twenty-first century, I'm afraid that for all too many it has become a job. As a calling or profession, education offers much. As a job, it offers little.

What is needed is the inclusion of the strong voices and good ideas of school people themselves about what constitutes a good learning environment for youngsters and how to develop such an environment. Even better would be school people working *with* "higher-ups" to devise the plan for school improvement. What is needed is an invitation to practitioners to bring a spirit of creativity and invention into the schoolhouse. What is needed is a sense of heart.

2

CULTURE IN QUESTION

> The illiterate of the twenty-first century will not be those who cannot read and write, but those who cannot learn, unlearn, and relearn.
>
> —*Alvin Toffler*

Probably the most important—and the most difficult—job of the school-based reformer is to change the prevailing culture of a school. The school's culture dictates, in no uncertain terms, "the way we do things around here." Ultimately, a school's culture has far more influence on life and learning in the schoolhouse than the state department of education, the superintendent, the school board, or even the principal can ever have.

The culture of a school is quite apparent to the newcomer. In one school, a new teacher stands up in a faculty meeting to express her views to the others on, say, pupil evaluation. Her contribution is received with mockery, cold stares, and put-downs: "Big deal. I've been doing that for twenty years." "Who does she think *she* is?" As the new teacher very quickly learns, the culture at her school dictates that newcomers must not speak until they have experienced, for at least two or three years, the toil of the old-timers. "That's the way we *do* things around here." And she learns that cruel and unusual punishments await those who violate the taboos of the school.

In another school, a high school student is tormented by his peers for studying on the day of the football game. And indeed, the culture in all too many secondary schools dictates that learning is not "cool" on Saturdays—or on any day of the week, for that matter.

In yet another school, a teacher encounters trouble managing a class full of difficult youngsters. Within a few days, every other teacher in the building knows of her problem—and volunteers to help. In the same school, when a student is experiencing difficulty with an assignment or a new concept, several fellow students step in to assist. "That's the way we do things around here."

The school culture is the complex pattern of norms, attitudes, beliefs, behaviors, values, ceremonies, traditions, and myths that are deeply ingrained in the very core of the organization. The culture is the historically transmitted pattern of meaning that wields astonishing power in shaping what people think and how they act.

Every school has a culture. Some are hospitable, others toxic. A school's culture can work for or against improvement and reform. Some schools are populated by teachers and administrators who are reformers, others by sheep, others by educators who are gifted and talented at subverting reform. Some school cultures are indifferent to reform.

And all school cultures are incredibly resistant to change. This is precisely why school improvement—from within or from without—is usually so futile. Yet unless teachers and administrators act to change the culture of a school, all "innovations" will have to fit in and around existing elements of the culture. That is, they will be superficial window dressing, incapable of making much of a difference.

To change the culture requires that we be first aware of the culture, the way things are here. This means crafting and using wide-angle, microscopic, and telescopic lenses, and honing our skills at observing. What do you see, hear, and experience in the school? What *don't* you see and hear? What are the indicators, the clues that reveal the school's culture? What behaviors get rewards and status here? Which ones are greeted with reprimand? Do the adults model the behavior they expect of youngsters? How do leaders react to critical situations? Who gets to make decisions? Do parents experience welcome, suspicion, or rejection when they enter the school?

Nondiscussables

An important part of awareness is attending to "nondiscussables." Nondiscussables are subjects sufficiently important that they get talked about frequently but are so laden with anxiety and taboos that these conversations take place only at the parking lot, the men's room, the playground, the car pool, or the dinner table at home. We are fearful that open discussion of these incendiary issues in polite society—at a faculty meeting, for example—will cause a meltdown. The nondiscussable is the elephant in the living room. Everyone knows this huge pachyderm is there, right between the sofa and the fireplace, and we go on mopping and dusting and vacuuming around it as if it did not exist.

Each school has its own nondiscussables. For one it is "the leadership of the principal." For another, "the way decisions get made here." For all too many it is "race" and "the underperforming teacher." Schools are full of these land mines from which trip wires emanate. We walk about carefully from day to day, trying not to detonate them. Yet by giving these nondiscussables this incredible power over us, by avoiding them at all cost, we issue that underperforming teacher a hunting license to continue this year as he did last year, taking a heavy toll on countless students and other teachers. We perpetuate poor leadership on the part of the principal, and we force ourselves to live with all the debilitating tensions that surround race.

The health of a school is inversely proportional to the number of its nondiscussables: the fewer the nondiscussables, the healthier the school; the more the nondiscussables, the more pathology in the school culture. And, of course, to change the culture of the school, its residents must name, openly acknowledge the existence of, and address the nondiscussables—especially the nondiscussables that impede learning.

Changing the Culture

It has been said that a fish would be the last creature on earth to discover water, so totally and continuously immersed in it is he. The same might be said of school people working within their culture. By the time that beginning teacher waits the obligatory three years to speak out in a faculty meeting, she too is likely to be so immersed in the culture that she will no longer be able to see with the clarity of a beginner important aspects of the school's culture, such as patterns of leadership, competition, fearfulness, self-interest, or lack of support.

To change the culture requires that we bring in more desirable qualities to replace the existing unhealthy elements of the culture. This is where possession of clear personal and collective visions is so important. Two educators, Saphier and King, identified a dozen healthy cultural norms: collegiality, experimentation, high expectations, trust and confidence, tangible support, reaching out to the knowledge bases, appreciation and recognition, caring celebration and humor, involvement in decision making, protection of what's important, traditions, and honest, open communications.[1] The authors believe that these qualities of a school's culture dramatically affect the capacity of a school to improve.

Thus, to change a school's culture requires the courage and skill not to remain victimized by the toxic elements of the school's culture but rather to address them. As one colleague put it, "How do I find the courage within myself to do what I must?" And, finally, culture building requires the skill to transform elements of the school's culture into forces that support rather than subvert the purposes of the school, even though, all the while, no one may be giving us "permission" to do so. Of course, all these acts of culture changing and culture building violate the very taboos of many school cultures themselves—*this* is why culture changing is the most important, most difficult, and most perilous job of school-based reformers. School cultures cannot be changed from without; they must be changed from within.

E. B. White, a fellow Maine gardener, once observed, "A person must have something to cling to. Without that we are as a peavine sprawling in search of a trellis." We educators are especially in need of a trellis, to keep us up off the ground in the face of the cold rains and hot winds that buffet the schoolhouse. In this chapter and the following, I'd like to consider with you what I believe is the trellis of our profession and the most critical element of any school's culture: an ethos hospitable to the promotion of human learning.

Learning Curves Off the Chart

It has been said that running a school is about putting first things first; leadership is determining what are the first things; and management is about putting them first. I would like to suggest that the "first thing," the most important feature of the job description for each of us educators, is to discover and provide the conditions under which people's learning curves go off the chart. Sometimes it's other people's learning curves: those of students, teachers, parents, administrators. But at all times it is our *own* learning curve.

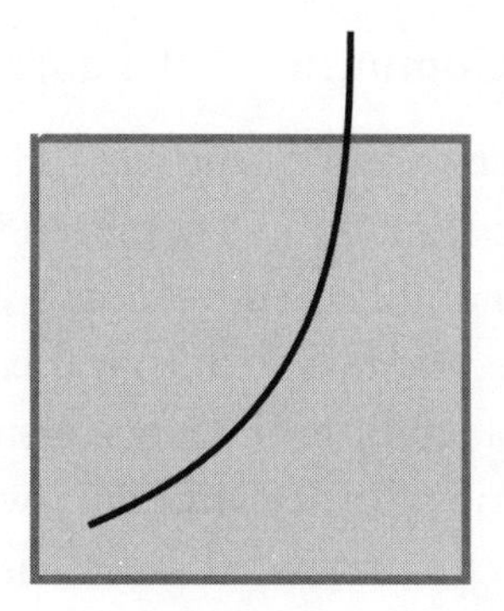

Schools exist to promote learning in all their inhabitants. Whether we are called teachers, principals, professors, or parents, our primary responsibility is to promote learning in others and in ourselves. That's what it means to be an educator. That's what sets us apart from insurance salesman, engineers, and doctors. To the extent our activities in school are dedicated to getting learning curves off the chart, I'd say what we do is a calling. To the extent that we spend most of our time doing something else in school, I'd say we are engaged in a job.

It is the ability to learn prodigiously from birth to death that sets humans beings apart from other forms of life. The greatest purpose of schools is to unlock, release, and foster this wonderful capability. T. H. White put it this way:

> "The best thing for disturbances of the spirit," replied Merlyn, beginning to puff and blow, "is to learn. That is the only thing that never fails. You may grow old and trembling in your anatomies, you may lie awake at night listening to the disorder in your veins, you may miss your only love and lose your monies to a monster, you may see the world about you devastated by evil lunatics, or know your honor trampled in the sewers of baser minds. There is only one thing for it, then—to learn. Learn why the world wags and what wags it. That is the only thing which the poor mind can never exhaust, never alienate, never be tortured by, never fear or distrust, and never dream of regretting. Learning is the thing for you."[2]

A Community of Learners

"Our school is a Community of Learners!" How many times do we see and hear this assertion, now so common in America's schools? For me it is both an ambitious, welcome vision and an empty promissory note. The vision is, first, that the school will be a *community*, a place full of adults and youngsters who care about, look after, and root for one another, and who work together for the good of the whole, in times of need as well as times of celebration.

Every member of a community holds some responsibility for the welfare of every other and for the welfare of the community as a whole. Schools face tremendous difficulty in fulfilling this definition of a community. More are organizations, institutions, or bureaucracies.

As if community were not ambitious enough, a community of learners is ever so much more. Such a school is a community whose defining, underlying culture is one of learning. The condition for membership in the community is that one learn, continue to learn, and support the learning of others. Everyone. A tall order to fill, and one to which all too few schools aspire and even fewer attain.

As I reflect back on the recent years of school reform, I interpret the meaning of this remarkable period in our nation's educational history as an invitation—nay, a demand—to examine every school policy, practice, and decision and ask of it the question, What, if anything, of importance is anyone learning as a consequence of doing *that?* Who learns what from ability grouping? Who learns what from letter grades of A, B, C? Who learns what from having twenty-six youngsters in a class? Who learns what from the annual practice of principals' evaluating teachers? God didn't create these and the myriad other school practices that now so clutter schools' cultures. *We* did—because at some time someone believed that this policy, practice, or procedure was capable of getting someone's learning curve off the chart.

A central responsibility of the school-based reformer is to take fresh inventory of these and other habituated practices so encrusted in our schools' cultures and to categorize them. Some, perhaps the practice of giving individual instruction or giving youngsters immediate feedback on their work, seem undeniably associated with promoting learning. They need to be retained. Others, such as ability grouping or parent nights, we may need to study; we need to become practitioner researchers and examine these practices to determine just what effect, if any, they are having on people's learning. Still other practices, perhaps faculty meetings or intrusive announcements over the loudspeaker, in many schools appear to contribute to no one's learning—may even impede learning—and need to be scrapped. A final category is for those activities that must continue to be carried out by a school, but in a more successful manner. We'll call this category "invent a better way."

Let me offer an example. Kim Marshall, a friend of mine and a principal in the Boston public schools, is a very conscientious staff developer, yet he was having a dreadful time with the time-consuming, anxiety-producing practice of annually evaluating teachers according to the system's protocol. He wrote, "Evaluation had become a polite, if near-meaningless matter between a beleaguered principal and a nervous teacher. . . . I had been trying to do a good job evaluating the 39 teachers at the Mather School, but I had to face the fact that my efforts were a sham. Were my evaluations of teachers having an impact on student learning? Very doubtful. Were they having an impact on teachers' learning? Precious little. My learning? No. Were they wasting everyone's time? You bet."

His attempts to connect teacher evaluations with someone's learning curve soaring revealed an educationally bankrupt practice deeply embedded in the culture of his school—and of his school system. Even so, for many reasons we can't just "scrap" the evaluation of teachers. It's important that all of us be evaluated from time to time, including school teachers (and authors!). Having discussed this nondiscussable and having carefully examined and categorized this sacrosanct school practice in terms of its capacity to promote learning, my friend found the courage to make some changes; he invented a better way.[3]

I believe that residing in all the stakeholders in schools—parents, teachers, students, principals—are wonderfully fresh, imaginative ideas about how to invent a better way. It takes moral outrage at ineffective practices, confidence that there *is* a better way, and the courage and invention to find it and put it into the place of what needs to be scrapped.

As noted earlier, all of us who work in and around schools now not only have the world's permission to take this inventory and act on the findings; the world is demanding these efforts of us. If this is the meaning of school reform, I'd say it is long overdue and to be welcomed by school practitioners. Whose learning curve goes off the chart by doing *that?* is a revolutionary question whose time has finally come.

At-Risk Students

I have observed over the years that unhealthy school cultures tend to beget "at-risk" students. One definition of an at-risk student that has special meaning for me is, "any student who leaves school before or after graduation with little possibility of continuing learning."

I remember visiting a high school just after the last spring exams and before graduation. As I approached the school grounds, I saw a group of students standing around a roaring fire, to which they were heartily contributing. I went over and asked, "What's up?"

"We're burning our notes and our books," replied one. "We're outta here!"

On further conversation, I learned that these students were not occupants of the bottom ability group, but rather A and B and C students, many headed for college.

That little incident continues to trouble me. I wonder how many students not so labeled are in fact at risk, with little possibility of continuing learning? How many graduate from our schools and exult in the belief that they have learned all they need or intend to know?

One reason why those youngsters were burning those books, literally, and why so many other youngsters burn their books, figuratively, at the conclusion of our treatment of them in schools is that, lurking beneath the culture of most schools (and universities) is a deadening message. It goes something like this: *Learn or we will hurt you.* We educators have taken learning, a wonderful, God-given, spontaneous capacity of all human beings, and coupled it with punitive measures. We have developed an arsenal of sanctions and punishments that we inextricably link with learning experiences. "Johnny, if you don't improve your multiplication tables, you're going to have to repeat fourth grade." "Mary, if you don't improve your compositions, I'm not going to write a favorable recommendation for college." "Sam, if you don't pass this next test, I'm calling your parents in." "Tom, if your state-administered standardized tests scores don't improve, you don't graduate." And so it goes. What the students burning their books are really saying is, "You can't hurt me any more." But so closely have we coupled learning and punishment that the students throw one into the fire with the other. School cultures in which students submit to learning, and to the threats of punishment for not learning, generate students who want to be finished with learning when they graduate from school. And, of course, this plays out for adults as well: the state tells the teacher or principal, "Unless you complete fifteen hours of continuing education credits this year, we will not renew your certification." Learn or we will hurt you.

A challenge of immense proportion to our profession is to find ways to uncouple learning and punishment. We must change the message from "Learn or we will hurt you" to "Learn or you will hurt yourself."

The Lifelong Learner

Why are these youngsters who literally or figuratively burn their books so much at risk? I read recently an estimate that fifty years ago, high school students graduated knowing perhaps 75 percent of what they would ever need to know to be successful in the workplace, the family, and the community. Today, the estimate is that graduates of our schools leave knowing perhaps 2 percent of what they will need to know in the years ahead—98 percent is yet to come. We all know the figures: knowledge doubles every three years; computer technology changes in eighteen months; the borders of Russia won't hold still. Yet today's graduates leave high school knowing far more than they ever did back in the fifties. The notion that we can acquire once and for all a basic kit of knowledge that will hold us in good stead for the rest of our lives is folly.

Business leaders tell us that the skills and abilities their employees will need in the twenty-first century include the following: teamwork, problem solving, interpersonal skills, oral communication, listening, personal development, creative thinking, leadership, goal setting, writing, organizational effectiveness, computation, and reading. Every one of these skills, of course, requires continual lifelong learning. The students who burn their books and their notes and celebrate the conclusion of their learning will be relegated to the periphery of the twenty-first century. And business leaders will continue to lament that they must spend $25 billion each year trying to teach recent graduates what they didn't learn in school.

Those who will thrive in the years ahead, in contrast, will be those who have, during the school experience, become active, voracious, independent lifelong learners—who will always be moving toward that 98 percent yet to come. The nature of the workplace, the nature of our society, and the nature of learning mean that we are all going to be expected to learn as we go along, or we won't survive.

I believe, therefore, that the most important requirement for graduation—whether from fourth, ninth, or twelfth grade—is some evidence that this youngster is becoming or has become an independent, lifelong learner. The telling questions to evaluate are, What evidence is there of enduring intellectual passion in this student? Is there evidence that this student is imbued with the qualities and capacities of the insatiable, lifelong learner? Is the student capable of posing questions, marshaling resources, and pursuing learning with dedication, independence, imagination, and courage?

So if your school has succeeded in getting 95 percent of its students scoring at the 95th percentile on standardized tests, and, at the same time, students are leaving a teacher, a grade, or the school "burning their books" saying "I'm done with this stuff; I'm outta here!" then you have won a battle and lost the war. The price of the short-term success is long-term failure. Enhancement of performance has led to a curtailment of learning. The school has failed in its most important mission. If the first major purpose of a school is to create and provide a culture hospitable to human learning, the second major purpose of a school is to make it likely that students and educators will become and remain lifelong learners.

These days, we use standardized tests to measure everything about everybody, from proficiency in pronouns to the causes of the Civil War. Yet it is disheartening to me that we have not identified as important nor attempted to measure to what extent our teachers, our classes, and our schools are turning out lifelong learners. When students arrive at school at age five, most carry within them the magical powers of lifelong learning. They are explorers, question-askers, inquirers, and risk-takers, and they are excited about finding answers. To paraphrase Pablo Picasso, every child is a learner. The problem is how to remain a learner once he grows up.

If we want to know how well we are doing with second or eighth graders in creating and sustaining lifelong learners, how do we find out? I doubt that standardized tests have much value in measuring or predicting the lifelong learner. There are better ways. One good way is to observe closely what students choose to do on their *own* time. After the bell rings at three o'clock—or on weekends, or over the summer—in what activities are youngsters engaged until bedtime? They will tell us. Are they going for walks in the woods, collecting and categorizing leaves and flowers and insects? Are they mapping their city street? Are they reading in the library? Are they campaigning for a local candidate? Are they learning to play a musical instrument? Or are they only watching television and hanging out? If it's true that character is what you do when no one is looking, then learning is what you do when you're not graded for it.

Asked seriously, the question, What do students do on their own time? reveals information that would probably alarm parents, educators, and the general public—as it should. When we come to believe that what our schools should be providing is a school culture that creates and sustains students' learning, that this is the trellis of our profession, then we will organize our schools, classrooms, and learning experiences differently. Show me a school whose inhabitants constantly examine the school's culture and work to transform it into one hospitable to sustained human learning, and I'll show you students who graduate with both the capacity and the heart for lifelong learning.

3

A COMMUNITY OF LEARNERS

> We must be the change we wish to see in the world. —*Mahatma Gandhi*

There are at-risk students. We might also introduce the concept of an at-risk educator: any teacher, principal, guidance counselor, or librarian who leaves school at the end of the day or the end of the year with little possibility of continuing learning.

At-Risk Educators

The imperiled place of learning in the lives of school practitioners is confirmed by staff developers with whom I speak. These are the educators whose job it is to promote adult learning curves. When I ask staff developers, "Who are the educators in our profession whose learning curves are off the chart?" most are quick to confide that it is the beginning teachers who are the voracious learners. A beginning teacher will go anywhere, observe, be observed, write, read, talk about practice—she is an insatiable learner. Staff developers offer that beginning administrators' learning curves are also steep, but not as steep as those of beginning teachers.

The learning curve of the beginning teacher remains high for two or three years. Then something curious seems to happen. The teacher finds some things that don't work very well and scraps them. And he finds some things that do work well, and he *enshrines* them. It's Halloween—out comes my Halloween folder. It's Martin Luther King Day—out comes my Martin Luther King folder. For the principal, it's out comes the "first faculty meeting of the year" folder, then the "first parent night of the year" folder, and then the "awards assembly" folder. Next September will be the same as last September. Once our practice is committed to a folder, once routinization and repetition replace invention, learning curves plummet.

Part of routine is, of course, about seeking comfort, security, and ease. Human nature seems to gravitate naturally that way. And to be sure, given the overwhelming demands placed on school people, it is impossible to create each activity anew. We must hold constant in some areas in order to find the time and energy to be creative in others.

Yet going on automatic pilot can have a devastating effect on the capacity of school people to be school-based reformers. For if you continue to do what you've always done, you'll always get what you've always got.

Staff developers also report that after perhaps a dozen years on the job, teachers (and principals), now beleaguered and depleted, stop showing up for voluntary staff development programs. They actively resist new opportunities to learn. You can build it, but they won't come! To make sure there are participants, much staff development thus has to be made mandatory. Veteran teachers and administrators do show up, but a curious body language accompanies them as they sit in the back rows: crossed arms, slouching posture, defiant facial expressions. They read or talk or engage in other activities. The message from participant to leader is clear: I dare you to try and teach me anything. At that point, educators have come not only to resist but to reject opportunities for new learning. Learning curves head further downward.

I remember attending a university commencement exercise. When degrees were conveyed to graduates from the medical school, the accompanying citation was, "We welcome you to a career of service and of learning." When graduates of the school of education were awarded their degrees, the citation read, "We welcome you to a career of service." A dagger to my heart! This oversight (I hope it was an oversight) presents an all-to-accurate epitaph for educators as learners. They have received, in that terrible phrase, their terminal degree.

We all know many educators in their forties, fifties, and sixties who continue to be insatiable learners. But the astonishing, disheartening, and unmistakable message for school people is this: Life under the roof of the schoolhouse is toxic to adult learning; the longer you reside there, the less learning is likely to occur. Alas, the learning curve of our profession looks like this:

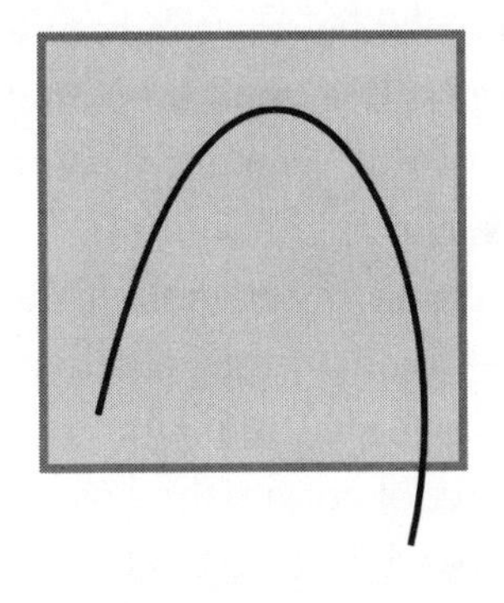

You Can Lead Where You Will Go

"Well," we say, "it's unfortunate that adults don't learn much in school—but, after all, the business of the school is to promote children's learning, not that of their teachers and administrators. The business of the educator is to serve, not to *be* served!" But I'm afraid it doesn't work that way. Ultimately there are two kinds of schools: learning-enriched schools and learning-impoverished schools. I've yet to see a school where the learning curves of the youngsters are off the chart upward while the learning curves of the adults are off the chart downward, or a school where the learning curves of the adults were steep upward and those of the students were not. Teachers and students go hand in hand as learners—or they don't go at all.

A major reason so many students are at risk as learners in our schools is that they are surrounded by so many at-risk educators. We routinely ask our youngsters, "What did you learn in school today?" It is every bit as important to ask ourselves, "What did *I* learn in school today?" What do we do in *our* spare time? Are we talking with colleagues about practice, visiting other classes, taking courses, maintaining a journal, reading—or watching TV, paying bills, and hanging out?

I'm familiar with one school—unquestionably a community of learners—where parents have agreed to replace the customary dinner-table question, "What did you learn in school today, Jimmy?" with "Let me tell you what I learned at work today"—studying in the lab, driving the bus, or baking the bread. Youngsters are fascinated that their parents still learn. And parents report this to be the most influential form of involvement available to them for stimulating their children's learning in school.

Children are not dumb. They look at the most important role models in their lives—their parents, teachers, principals, and ministers—and say, "I want to be like *that*." If they see adult models who are done, baked, cooked, finished as learners, they too want to be done, baked, cooked, finished as learners—"I'm outta here!" If they see about them adults who ask questions, read, write, pose and solve problems, work together, and struggle with important learning, *they* want to ask questions, read, write, pose and solve problems, and engage in and struggle with important learning. That's why a parent's reading to a youngster can be so powerful to the child's learning: this twosome is a small yet powerful community of learners in which both parties engage together in learning.

It's interesting, in this context, to consider the common instructions given by flight attendants to airline passengers: In the event of an oxygen failure, those of you traveling with small children should first place the oxygen mask on your own face and *then*, and only then, place the mask on your child's face.

Recently I asked a flight attendant why the airline and the FAA require this ritual. I learned something. The flight attendant replied, "Of course, the adult must be alive in order to be of any help in keeping the youngster alive." She added that adults are a bunch of "rescuers." If a child is in distress we go immediately, instinctively to the rescue. She said, "Unless we remind them, it's very difficult to get adults to tend to themselves before they attend to their children." And then she added something else: "The oxygen mask is grotesque and frightening to many children. Youngsters are taught not to put plastic bags over their heads, and now here we are expecting them to do just that. They won't do it. However, if the trusted adult role model first dons the oxygen mask, the youngster will follow suit." New learning is, of course, just as scary as a new oxygen mask.

Tragically, schools are all too full of "corpses" who faithfully, persistently, heroically each day place oxygen masks on youngsters' faces, while they themselves are anoxic. A school is no different than a 757; if we want youngsters to put on the oxygen mask of learning, we adults must do it first, and right alongside them. Elizabeth Cady Stanton put it wisely: "Self-development is a higher duty than self-sacrifice."

As I visit schools, I find them populated with two quite distinct classes of citizens. The first class comprises the adults who are learn*ed*. We have certification, degrees, and diplomas. We're anointed. The priesthood. We've done it. We're finished. The second class of citizens is composed of learn*ers*. These are the students. The business of most schools seems to be for the learn*ed* to transmit as much learning to the learn*ers* as we can from September to June.

I shudder to recall my early days as principal when, after getting a staff development activity going for the teachers on, say, the use of manipulative math materials, I would tiptoe unobtrusively out the back of the room and go back to my office to shuffle papers, answer phone messages, and attend to "more important matters." Looking back on it now, I see that my behavior was hardly unobtrusive. What I was telegraphing to teachers every other Thursday afternoon was the undermining message, "Learning is for unimportant people; important people don't need to learn." Well, everyone wants to be important! If being an important person is to be immune from learning, it's a wonder there are *any* learners in schools—youngsters or adults.

I'm afraid I frequently see the same message conveyed to principals by their superintendents who get the workshop started and then tiptoe out the back of the room and leave to attend to their "more important" matters. Contrast this with the superintendent and deputy superintendent in District 2 in New York City who are creating a school *system* culture hospitable to adult learning. Indeed, continual learning on the part of all educators in the system is expected, demanded, facilitated, and rewarded. For example, each principal is paired with and frequently visits and observes another principal. The craft knowledge of each educator is made visible and exchanged with others. And teacher and administrator are evaluated according to this commitment to their own learning.

We would all do well to heed the words of Goethe: "Things which matter most must never be at the mercy of things which matter least." For an educator, what matters are *more* important than learning and making our learning visible to others? I think the most honorable, fitting title any educator—teacher, principal, or professor—can assume is that of "leading learner" or "head learner." For when the adults in the schoolhouse commit to the heady, hearty, and difficult goal of promoting their own learning as well as that of their colleagues and students, several things follow: by leaving the ranks of the senior, wise priesthood—the learned—these individuals become first-class members of the community of learners; they build community; and when they come to take their own learning seriously, to value and promote it, so will students take *their* learning seriously. In a lovely piece of writing, one elementary school teacher put it this way: "Learning isn't something like chicken pox, a childhood disease that makes you itch for awhile, and then leaves you immune for the rest of your life."

Having taught in some universities and been a student in many, I find the pedagogy in most rather primitive—lecture and discussion. But one thing needs to be said for universities as communities of learners: the teachers constantly display and model, even flaunt, their own learning. Students read what their teachers have written, join research teams with their teachers, and hear their teachers disclose what problems they are wrestling with and how they are going about addressing them. I believe that by being alive and visible as learners, university teachers have their most profound influence on the present and subsequent learning of their students. It is infectious. I wish the same could be said of K–12 teachers.

Allow me to share a dream. What if schools and universities were not two places, occasionally intersecting, but instead one place where teaching, learning, research, and community service were occurring all the time? What if human beings from preschool to postgraduate school occupied the same geographical location and constituted an intergenerational community of inquiry? What if we refused to accept the given that there must be two distinct cultures and instead created anew one culture, a community of learners? What if every citizen of this "school" were committed to the same goals: to be a lifelong learner, to discover new knowledge, to help design and construct the learning organization, to share in the decision making, and to live and work as colleagues? How much more likely would it be that young people would become lifelong learners if they could each day observe, experience, and work with adults who were lifelong learners? How much more would teachers and youngsters learn if they were part of a culture replete with role models of the reflective practitioner, scholar, and researcher? How much more would the older scholars learn from the persistent presence of the younger scholars? And how much more relevant would the scholarship be? Research would be everyone's work. The ten-year-old researching the inhabitants of pond water, the doctoral student researching the inhabitants of pond water, and the professor doing the same would become colleagues in researching pond water. The meaning of *teacher* and of *student* would never again be seen in the same way. Nor would the pond water.

The important message I am suggesting here is captured beautifully in a bumper sticker I have on my car: "You can't lead where you won't go." Our business as educators is to lead young people toward profound and lasting levels of learning. We can't do that unless we go there ahead of them, behind them, and alongside them. If this message is the bad news, the good news is, "You *can* lead where you *will* go."

The Leading Learners

Why is it so crucial that teachers and administrators become the leading learners in their schools? The first reason is the extraordinary power of modeling. "Do as I do, as well as I say" is a powerful message not lost on youngsters who want to emulate the most important adult role models in their lives. Second, the world is changing. The problem with schools isn't that they are no longer what they once were; the problem is that they are precisely what they once were. The world around the schoolhouse is changing dramatically. Teaching and leading are not innate for most of us. We teach and lead better when we constantly learn how to teach and lead. I found these words of Eric Hoffer, a San Francisco longshoreman philosopher, on a huge sign at the door of a school in Connecticut: "In times of change, learners inherit the earth, while the learned find themselves beautifully equipped to deal with a world that no longer exists."

Third, with learning comes replenishment of body, mind, and spirit—and of schools. These days, schools and the educators who reside in them are depleted. Replenishment comes from either leaving the exhausting work of the schoolhouse or from remaining there and coming alive as a learner. In order not to lose educators from the schools as dropouts, they must be restored as learners. The self-renewal of educators and the self-renewal of our schools go hand in hand. One is dependent on the other.

Some thirty years ago, Ron Edmonds introduced us to the words, "All children can learn." At the time, many educators and parents thought the idea that all children can learn was an unrealistic dream. It was believed that some children can learn all things, all children can learn some things, but all children cannot learn all things. Today most educators have come not only to utter and accept Edmonds's words but also to actually believe them and act on them.

Let me make an even more outrageous assertion: all educators can learn. Even that burned-out forty-year veteran and that "brain dead" one up on the third floor. To hold low expectations for them and their capacity as learners is just as destructive and corrosive as believing that those youngsters on the other side of the tracks cannot learn. The question for the educator is not *whether* all humans can learn but what conditions we can devise so that they *will* learn. For only when the schoolhouse becomes a context for adult development will it become hospitable to student development.

I believe that schools can become much more than places where there are big people who are learn*ed* and little people who are learn*ers*. They can become cultures where youngsters are discovering the joy, the difficulty, and the excitement of learning and where adults are continually *re*discovering the joy, the difficulty, and the excitement of learning. Places where we are all in it together—learning by heart.

4

INFORMATION RICH AND EXPERIENCE POOR

> Almost everyone has had occasion to look back upon his school days and wonder what became of the information he was supposed to have amassed during his years of schooling.
>
> —*John Dewey*

Much rides on the adults becoming insatiable learners in our schools. Pupils' present and subsequent learning depends on it. And so, therefore, does school-based reform. A community of learners is a collection of youngsters and grown-ups working together to provide and sustain their own and one another's learning. But just how do we make good on the promises implicit in the statement, "Our school is a community of learners"?

I would like to suggest conditions under which adults and youngsters in schools can come alive as learners. These are also the conditions under which teachers and administrators can find continual renewal in their work and develop a culture of learning and reform within their schools. As we know, learning is a complex and often mysterious process. Attempting to illuminate the ways learning can happen is equally complex and mysterious.

A friend of mine is a staff developer in Texas. She introduced me to a new phrase I have added to my educational jargon: *sit 'n' git*. As in, "We'll come in, have some coffee and Danish, then sit down for some sit 'n' git with Roland Barth, or someone. Then we'll have a break and come back for some more sit 'n' git until lunch. After which we'll continue with the sit 'n' git until we go home at three o'clock."

John Goodlad and others who have carefully observed classrooms in our nation's schools estimate that 85 percent of the time the prevailing pedagogy follows this format: the teacher talks, the students listen, with teacher-directed discussion occasionally interspersed. In elementary schools, middle and junior high schools, and high schools (and in colleges and universities, I might add), large-group, didactic instruction—sit 'n' git—prevails.

The Transmission of Knowledge Model

The organizing principle of most pedagogy in most schools can be depicted by what we might call the *Transmission of Knowledge* model, as shown in Figure 4.1.

This model assumes the existence of an accumulated body of knowledge (K), usually encoded in written language. Knowledge is stored, from Plato to nuclear physics, in the Library of Congress. The proper business of schools is to transmit as much of this knowledge to students as possible. The proper function of students is to learn as much of this knowledge as efficiently as possible between September and June and to display its acquisition upon demand of authorities, usually through standardized tests. Students are evaluated according to how much K they have acquired and how quickly, and how able they are to demonstrate this acquisition. The model

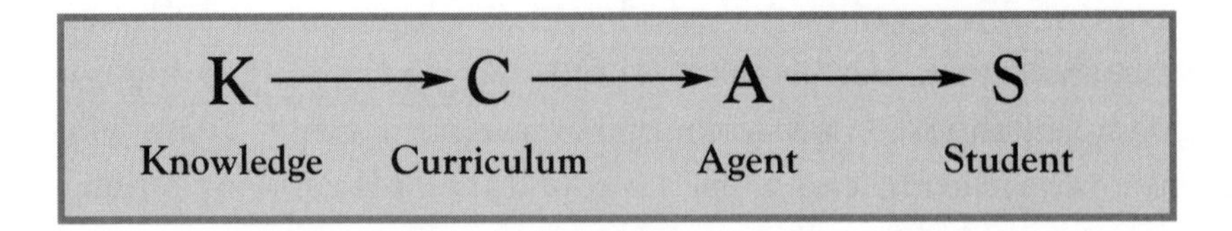

Figure 4.1. Transmission of Knowledge Model of Learning

assumes the primacy of didactic teaching and the central role of language in the learning process.

Because all of accumulated knowledge is too vast to be conveyed to students, educators select those parts that they consider most crucial and appropriate for children of different ages to "know": the great explorers in the fifth grade, algebra in eighth, U.S. history in twelfth, and so on. This subset of K packaged for the teacher is called the curriculum (C).

Whether it emanates from the state or local board of education, the superintendent, or the principal, the curriculum is then transmitted to an agent (A), who in turn transmits it to the students (S). The agent is usually a teacher but might also be a computer program or a television set.

The Transmission of Knowledge model is a venerable one, built upon important assumptions about knowledge, curriculum, learning, and the role of the teacher. Most schools and most teachers are as wedded to this model today as they were a hundred years ago. It's how *they* learned. It directs their actions from day to day.

One of the central reasons for the incredible persuasiveness and pervasiveness of the Transmission of Knowledge model is that it allows learning to be evaluated and numbers attained. And then people can be held accountable. How many state capitals did Johnny know in September? How many in June? How many causes of the Civil War? The differential tells us how much his teacher has taught and how much Johnny has learned. And, as we know, everyone feeds off these numbers.

Problems with Sit 'n' Git

When we look at how students respond to our attempts to transmit to them these vast amounts of knowledge, we find that the model seems to have some unintended effects: for example, about 71 percent of American high school students admit that they have cheated on an exam the previous year.[1] Many students may feel that the only way they can demonstrate competence in such an overwhelming body of knowledge is to cheat.

The Transmission of Knowledge model may be successful at generating numbers and holding students and teachers "accountable." Yet it is beset with tragic flaws. First of all, it is *futile* to try to transmit to students everything we think they should know. One study concluded that *nine* additional years of schooling would be required for students to master all the material recommended by the various national organizations that have put forth standards. In addition, researchers—and our experience—suggest that as learners, we retain in six weeks perhaps 5 percent of what we are taught in this way. (Retention goes up to perhaps 7 or 8 percent if audiovisual aids are employed.) In two years the recall is inconsequential. Transmitting knowledge from the person who has it to the person we want to have it is clearly a weak treatment. We say so often, "I don't have *time* to teach the youngsters [or their teachers] all they need to know." It's like driving a car that gets three miles per gallon—in an oil crisis.

Last summer, while cleaning out the attic of my Maine farmhouse, I came across a cardboard box labeled "Princeton." Forty years ago, I filed in that box all my notes from four years of college, along with syllabi and final examinations. I stored this material carefully, even reverentially. This was my college education, for which I had waited on tables for four years by day and labored in the library for four years by night.

For the fun of it, I opened up the box and took out some folders. Despite three-hour lectures for sixteen weeks each, I couldn't even remember *taking* many of these courses. I then administered to myself a couple of final exams. I'd have been very happy to settle for 0.5 percent retention. I found none. Try it with your box!

When I was done, I had no difficulty agreeing with what one observer had to say about that art form known as the lecture: "Lecturing is an unnatural act, an act for which providence did not design humans. It is perfectly all right now and then to speak while others remain silent, but to do so regularly, one hour at a time, for one person to drone on and on while others sit in silence, I do not believe that this is what the Creator designed humans to do."

Another flaw in the Transmission of Knowledge model is that it does not—and cannot—engage the learner very fully or for very long. Each of us carries, I believe, a profound human need to experience not just learning but activity and joy in learning. Not all the time, to be sure, but at least some of the time. I remember vividly my first position in our profession: teaching third grade in a public elementary school in Massachusetts. I discovered very soon that after about ten minutes of me talking, the students were hanging from the lights. I learned that if I was to teach them I would have to get them interested and involved. Subsequently, I discovered when teaching at Harvard that after about ten minutes of me talking, *grown-ups* were hanging from the lights. (Adults do it differently and usually more politely: they start to plan the weekend chores or the menu for a dinner party or the shopping list.) Nowadays, after about ten minutes a little alarm goes off in my head. It says, "Stop talking, get them involved, or forget it."

Schools, wedded to the Transmission of Knowledge model, don't meet very well the needs of little or big people to be involved and engaged as learners. Indeed, to "succeed" in transmitting knowledge to many students, we must medicate them with Ritalin (85 percent of the world's Ritalin users are in the United States), Prozac, and other pharmacological treatments. Even then, so-called attention deficit disorders abound in our schools.

The model just doesn't fit many children's learning styles. We can devise better means of promoting learning than by talking, and we can provide more active involvement than listening. I believe that when we do, students and adults will leave school, not burning their books, but with a good possibility that they will continue to learn.

I find our education system akin to a radio that seems to play on but one station, WDTT—Didactic Teacher Talk. As teachers, we can adjust the volume, the tone, and the length of the program. As students, we can employ the on or off switch whenever

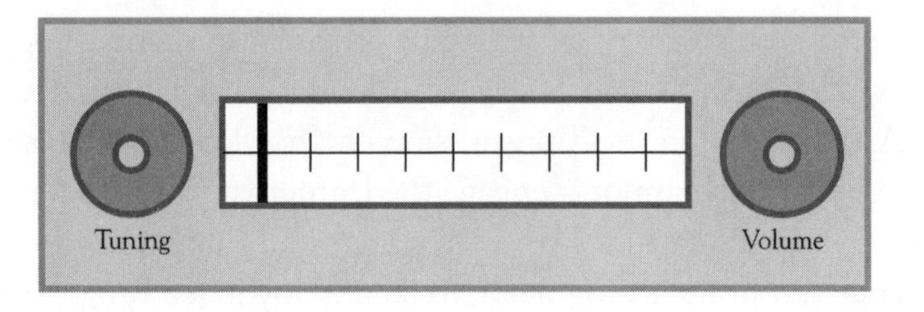

we choose. But I do not believe that as a profession we have yet discovered where the tuning knob *is*, let alone how to explore different stations with it. There can be no community when one person is talking all the time and the rest are presumed to be listening. And, as we have seen, there can be little long-term learning for either teacher or student. In short, by confining our pedagogy to Station WDTT, we deprive students and teachers of *both* community and learning.

Exploring Other Stations

If I could rub the lamp and ask the genie to grant a single wish that would reform our schools, it would be to reverse the ratio. Instead of 85 percent teacher talk and 15 percent something else, it would be 15 percent teacher talk and 85 percent something else.

But what do you *do* with them during all that time if you aren't lecturing? What's the something else? When teachers and administrators begin to ask *that* question, they become school-based reformers. Hey, it's risky out there when you leave the sit 'n' git station—as many teachers who now work with block scheduling and intensive learning know. They must instruct a group of youngsters not for fifty-five minutes but for two hours!

I know how risky it is. There are times—probably many times—when each of us has taken the risk of departing from sit 'n' git in the name of promoting students' learning. Sometimes taking these risks has devastating consequences. I recall when I taught a little elective class of sixth graders the use of Boston's public transportation system, the MBTA. Instead of conventional instruction about

Boston's neighborhoods using maps and books, each week we hopped on the subway and explored on foot the area around a different T station in Boston. Then one day I lost two youngsters somewhere in the vicinity of Cleveland Circle Reservoir. The rest is history—and so is that little elective class.

But I have a more hopeful story to tell. A few years ago, I vowed to myself that I would never again accept an invitation to give a talk or offer a workshop if it meant only that I talked and others listened. I don't believe in it. My new resolve led to a good deal of both worry and invention as I sought to find different ways to involve participants through writing, small- and large-group conversation, body movements, team-building activities, and other means. For two years I was able to fulfill my pledge to myself.

And then I agreed to receive an honorary degree—and, by the way, give a graduate school commencement speech to twenty-five hundred students, their parents, and faculty! Graduation is, of course, a setting that cries out for the didactic delivery of a few wise and witty ideas. How do you *involve* all these folks for twenty-five minutes? Do I dare to even try?

I was terrified. I persevered. I worried all winter. Finally, with the coaching of a friend and teacher educator, I devised a plan to frame and then pose a handful of probing questions. I invited each graduate (and professor and parent) to reflect on her higher education and then, in conversation with the person seated beside her, to summarize in sixty seconds her response to each of the questions.[2] Talk about classroom and time management skills!

I am delighted—and relieved—to report that we all risked violation of expectation and pulled it off with great engagement, humor, novelty, and even a sense of community. And, I suspect, with some new learning all the way round. My final words to the group were, "Unlike the case with most graduation speakers, you will remember who spoke at yours. *You* did!" And many of the conversations lasted well afterward. This frightening and exhilarating experience confirmed my belief that if we are insistent and persistent, we can *always* involve the learners in constructing and participating in their own learning. And they will always learn more from the experience. And it will always be risky.

Who Poses the Questions?

We cannot build a school culture hospitable to human learning by relying 85 percent of the time on the Transmission of Knowledge model. Once we get off the sit 'n' git station, we may find many blank spaces on that radio dial with no sounds at all; there may be lewd music on other stations, lots of static on others, and much that is unknown. Yet the most powerful signals await us on these other stations, signals capable of promoting both community and profound learning.

In schools, adults almost always pose the questions that students are supposed to answer: characterize Hamlet's mother, analyze the effects of the Industrial Revolution on the farms. Students, in turn, invariably comply. Or don't. Observers find that schools run according to the Transmission of Knowledge model succeed in training youngsters to submit to adult authority and to substitute adult problems, objectives, tasks, and ideas for their own. Sometimes they reject knowledge, teachers, and school—literally or figuratively burning their books. And sometimes they act out—as a comment from my heroic, long-enduring fourth-grade teacher reminds me: "Roland and I have had a little talk about respect for authority. I am certain this promising student will get better citizenship reports from now on."

An urban high school youngster says it best:

> And then at the end of my sophomore year I just stopped going, man. I hated school anyway. I always hated it. One reason was because I didn't have any patience. I wanted to do what I wanted to do. And other than that, school was just . . . boring! I mean, you sit up in a hot classroom, and the teachers are mean, and they're old, you know what I mean. Once I got past kindergarten and first grade when we did all the activities and made stuff—once it be-

> came more book work, I just didn't like it. It's like this—let's say you don't know how to drive a car and I'm gonna teach you. I can say, "well, you're gonna have to do this, you're gonna have to press down on the brake, and throw it in drive." But after awhile, I can't do too much more talking. You're gonna have to get behind the wheel and do it yourself. And I think that's how school should be. Instead of being told how to do things, you have to do it more yourself. I mean, after telling me the basics, shut up—let me do it now. That's just how I am.[3]

A study recently conducted by the Educational Testing Service supported this student: "Students whose teachers conducted hands-on learning activities outperformed their peers by about 70 percent of a grade level in math and 40 percent of a grade level in science."[4]

Some call acquired knowledge that doesn't *go* anywhere *inert knowledge*. Our schools are replete with inert knowledge. Despite the (now waning) educational rhetoric that boasts expressions like *discovery*, *inner motivation*, *exploration*, *active involvement*, and *best interests of the child*, school continues to be an adult-centered, not student-centered, enterprise. And the greater the preoccupation with standardized tests, the more adult-centered it becomes. It is no surprise that many youngsters' natural excitement and curiosity about the world are more thwarted than nurtured by the school experience.

For a telling indicator of a school's culture, a visitor might ask the following questions: Who poses the questions that occupy students and adults here? How much of the time are students responding to problems posed by others and how much to problems they pose for themselves? How much of the faculty's staff development is built around problems and questions posed by others and how much by problems and questions they pose for themselves?

The adult development literature suggests that we grown-ups engage most heartily in our own learning, learn more, and care most about our learning when we pose our own questions. Right now, for example, the question I'm posing for myself is how to get back into a little sea kayak when I have capsized in deep water. I am alive as a learner. (And I hope will continue to be so as a paddler!) If I were to inflict this question on someone else, it would probably present a far less rich learning opportunity.

And so it is with students. I have heard many criticisms of public schools. Some I agree with, some I don't. The most apt criticism of schools I have ever heard is that schools are information rich and experience poor. Students and teachers are swamped by information—from sit 'n' git lectures; from the computer; from TV; from the written word in books, workbooks, and worksheets. We confine students in forty-by-forty-foot cubicles all day long, where they deal with symbols and abstractions. Students are told about oceans, animals, cities, farms, societies; they read about them and examine pictures of them. All the while, the oceans, animals, cities, farms, and societies are right outside the classroom doors! Experiencing primary source materials will always generate more learning than will working with secondary sources.

To be sure, school people are subject to severe pressures to remain within the classroom cubicles and to stick with sit 'n' git. They face strong opposition when they go out into the world: field trips cost money; internships need supervision and demand a great deal of careful planning; discipline problems may emerge that can only be kept in check within the school. Bringing experiences into the classroom can be daunting, and doing so risks loss of control. The scope and sequence and the pressures to pass the next state standardized exam allow little enough time, as it is, to prepare. Yet if we are really committed to developing communities of learning, we must engage in activities that have the capacity to build community and to promote learning and a lifetime love of learning.

5

EXPLORATION

> You cannot discover new oceans unless you risk losing sight of the shore. —*Anonymous*

One of my passions is sailing. Let me share some of my sailing experiences, and we'll see what we can learn from them as metaphors for learning.

For forty years I have sailed the salt waters of San Francisco Bay, Muscongus Bay, and Florida Bay. For about the same number of years, I have been a student, a teacher, and a principal in schools and universities. So you might say I am a sailor interested in education and an educator interested in sailing.

I doubt that any sailors have pursued their passion for very long without experiencing some powerful new learnings—about seamanship and navigation; about meteorology; about limitations of self, others, and the vessel; about relationships; and about winds, rocks, fog, and currents. Boats, especially sailing craft, are remarkable learning environments.

In sailing I find abundant opportunities to take risks (happily hedged by various forms of safety devices) and to face a never-ending supply of novelty and surprise. It is in sailing that I experience a sense of adventure and purposeful activity. It is in sailing that I learn to get along with others and to share leadership—or else live with the very real consequences of going it alone. It is in sailing that I actively engage in solving problems. It is in sailing that I experience a sense of contribution, by sharing the natural world with others and by helping them learn to sail. It is in sailing that I find the joy and freedom which accompany hard work that doesn't feel either hard or like work. And, above all, it is in sailing that I assume responsibility for an important portion of my own life and for the lives of others.

These, for me, are the conditions that come with life aboard that curious vessel that is half bird and half fish, the sailboat. And these are the very same conditions, I believe, that prompt learning in such an unending supply in other settings as well.

Boats and Schools

So if the job of a school is to promote learning, I think a good school should be more like a boat, even a leaky old boat. There is much to learn at sea. Look, for instance, at the powerful learning that occurs under the roofs of boat-building apprentice shops in Rockport and Kennebunkport, Maine, or in Newburyport, Massachusetts, where apprentices proudly learn skills in the context of finishing off a boat, and where evaluation comes, incontrovertibly, at the launching. And look at what are known as sail-training vessels where, in the time-honored tradition, students spend from two hours to two years before the mast. Many of the Outward Bound schools throughout the world offer these kinds of formative experiences as well.

I dare say there is no youngster or adult who has undergone a prolonged maritime experience who could not cite a half-dozen huge learnings and whose life has not in some way been transformed by them. These life-altering passages have a lasting effect that makes much of what is learned (or not learned) in school seem meager by comparison. Indeed, the Hurricane Island Outward Bound school boasts, "What you learn here you learn forever." It may not always be forever, but I'm sure it's more than 5 percent in six weeks, and it isn't then relegated to a box in the attic.

Ask my daughters. On the drive over to Rockland, Maine, to board the *Bowdoin*, a famous eighty-eight-foot Arctic exploring schooner, then under the command of Outward Bound, one of them asked, "Do you think they'll let us help sail before we get to Gloucester?" This famous fishing port lay a good two days before us. Well, before we cleared Rockland Harbor, Carolyn, my fifteen-year-old, stood her watch, alone at the helm (taller than she is) of the largest sailing ship she had ever been aboard. Recently, Carolyn reflected on this experience, now a dozen years past:

> As a child I was frequently asked to perform any sailing chore needed out on the bowsprit of our Friendship sloop. I took great pride in this because no one else seemed to want the frightening, and often dangerous, task of crawling out over a slippery bowsprit, hand over hand, from stay to stay, in order to furl or unfurl a balky jib. Alone, a small girl out on the bowsprit, with the waves crashing beneath me, I felt complete and invincible.
>
> On the *Bowdoin* I had a transforming experience up there in the bow. It was in the middle of a gale, and I, always the youngest and the smallest, was as usual furling a headsail. All of a sudden, a great wave (often called a widow maker) crashed over the bow. I lost my hold on the sail. I struggled to regain my connection to the slippery deck and found nothing. I felt my small body sliding with the wave toward the all-too-low toe rail. I pictured myself sloshing overboard into the boiling—and frigid—Atlantic. Then, I felt a strong hand grab the back straps of my foul weather pants. The power of the wave was countered by an unknown human's strength behind me.
>
> One lasting learning from this moment on the *Bowdoin* is of the power and true danger of the sea. After this, I never quite regained a feeling of fearlessness or invincibility out on the bow of any boat.
>
> There was a second, and perhaps more important and lasting, learning from this moment. This experience remains in my memory as my first step in a lifelong learning process of attempting to understand that I am not alone in this world and that I need not

bear all of life's risks alone. I learned that I need other human beings and can be saved by my connection to them and by their connection to me.

Information Rich and Experience Rich

But, you say, not every youngster (especially one landlocked in Topeka or Atlanta) can manage two years at a boat-building shop, four weeks on an Outward Bound pulling boat, or a long passage on the *Bowdoin*. Let's look again at the characteristics of the seafaring world that seem to promote such fecund learning: risk-taking with abundant safety harnesses; novelty and a sense of adventure and purposefulness; posing our own questions; hard work, joy, and freedom; collective learning and leadership; engagement and responsibility for our own lives and for the lives of others. An increasing number of land-based schools demonstrate that it is quite possible to introduce into the culture of the schoolhouse each of these characteristics so essential to learning.

For instance, the Metropolitan Center (MET), a high school in Providence, Rhode Island, integrates school-based learning and work-based learning—academics and experience. Students at the MET don't attend classes in the traditional sense. Each one of them confronts the question, What do I really want to learn about? Then a curriculum is attached to the aspiration of the student. There are no classes, no textbooks, no hall passes, no grades. Students work one-on-one and in groups of a dozen or so with an adviser who is responsible for helping them identify an experience in the city and then develop and carry out an individual learning plan.

Each student spends several days a week immersed in a carefully supervised internship in the Providence area. For instance, one young Latina woman served as an interpreter at a children's hospital emergency ward. Underlying these experiences is a small list of academic goals common to all students, whether they work in a horse stable, a nail salon, an art gallery, or a hospital emergency ward. But the academic program is driven foremost by what students want to learn and are learning—and find they need to learn—at the work site.

Students are continually assessed on the basis of exhibitions, portfolios, and oral and written examinations, often before a panel that frequently includes employers, parents, and other students, as well as faculty. This rigorous evaluation process clearly supports high levels of students learning. Of the first class of forty-four mostly inner-city graduates, 90 percent are going on to college.

Another example is City on a Hill Charter School, where, in a real sense, Boston has become the curriculum. Ninth, tenth, eleventh, and twelfth graders fan out to serve eighty community organizations throughout the city, contributing two or three days a week in schools, courts, city and state offices, and businesses. The average daily attendance is 93 percent. The school has high standards, which these work sites help youngsters achieve. "The real world is a wonderful reinforcer of some of the values we promote," observes cofounder Sarah Kass. "When a supervisor says, 'Tuck in your shirt and spit out your gum,' it has a different weight coming from the workplace than coming from us." Last year, 100 percent of these inner-city youngsters graduated and earned acceptance to college.

For example, two students, working together as guides at the Boston Aquarium, were responsible for responding to a barrage of questions from visiting children and adults about the hundreds of different aquatic creatures, from giant sharks to tiny sea horses. Of course, the students now had a compelling reason to learn all they could about this marine environment.

There is the Eagle Rock School in Colorado, where, before they matriculate, all new secondary students spend three weeks out in the mountains, hiking, rock climbing, and developing skills in teamwork, perseverance, and leadership, skills they will take with them to their school.

It is interesting to note that many of these remarkable, experiential learning environments are *elementary* schools. At the Mission Hill Elementary Pilot School in Boston, for example, young children pose and then explore many of their own important questions. There are a growing number of elementary schools associated with Expeditionary Learning Outward Bound. This is one of the most successful of the programs spawned by the New American Schools Development Corporation in 1992 in an attempt to create "break the mold" schools. For these schools, the out-of-doors is as much a part of the classroom as the indoors.

And then there are the several hundred MicroSociety Schools, which successfully replicate for elementary students key elements of society—judicial systems, businesses, banks, stores, post offices—inside the schoolhouse. One visitor, Lee Iacocca, observed, "Other kids do arithmetic in workbooks, you've done it in your own banks and stores; other kids just read newspapers, you've produced them." Another observer commented, "You haven't heard anything until you've heard a third-grader complain about his income taxes!" Matthew, a sixth grader, had this to say about his MicroSociety school experience:

> When I was in fifth grade I was the Loan Officer of the bank. I had never used a spreadsheet on a computer and I wasn't familiar with the loan application. It took me two months. Then in sixth grade, I was President of the IRS and had to learn all the jobs and all the forms in case one of my employees was absent and I had to take over their job. I also had to double check all the work of the younger kids, especially the kindergartners.
>
> If you don't do something in regular school you only affect yourself. But if you don't do something in Micro, your whole company is affected. If you don't put the proper entries in the computer you don't just hurt the person who owns the bank account, you hurt the whole school.[1]

Building a community of learners, indeed.

In the experiences of students in these schools we see examples of all the critical elements of learning I have experienced in my sailing career. For example:

The student serving as an interpreter in a Providence hospital emergency ward found herself taking risks in an environment full of unpredictability; by communicating accurate, critical information, she assumed responsibility for her own life and for the lives of others, which certainly provided a sense of adventure, purpose, and service.

The two students who partnered as guides at the Boston Aquarium learned a great deal about getting along with others and about sharing leadership. By facing, each day, a new bunch of tourists who asked unexpected questions, the students experienced novelty and surprise as well as joy and freedom in their hard work; they also contributed to the experience of the tourists.

The sixth grader who served as president of the IRS likewise found himself taking risks and actively engaging in solving problems; by learning all the forms and all of the jobs of his staff, he assumed responsibility for himself and for others; he too experienced a sense of adventure and purposefulness.

An old fishing captain in Maine once observed, "Knowledge earned is better than knowledge learned—if it don't come too dear." It is time for students in school to cease being force-fed and to earn their knowledge, even if it may occasionally come too dear. Let's allow ourselves to celebrate the profound opportunities for learning that exist in endless supply outside the classroom and those we can bring into the classroom.

Experiential Learning: Another Model

Embedded in these experiences is another model of learning that stands in juxtaposition to the Transmission of Knowledge model. The *Experiential* model of learning might look something like Figure 5.1.

This model assumes that knowledge is unique to each individual and that a person comes to know most from direct, personal exploration of his environment. Learning comes from the interaction between the student (S) and the real world (RW), be

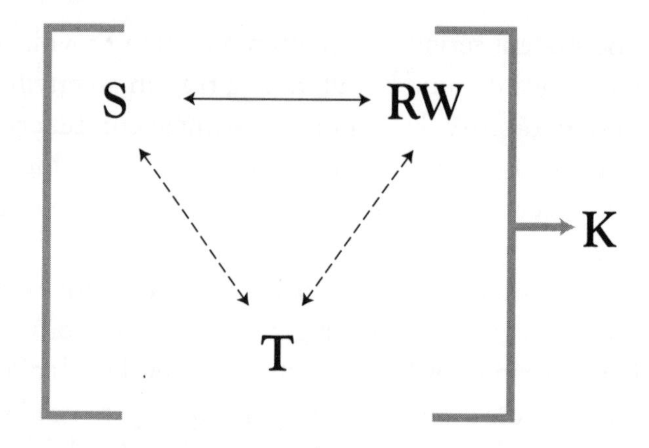

Figure 5.1. Experiential Model of Learning

it an idea, a person, or a swinging pendulum. The teacher (T) in the model occupies a different place in the learning process. The Outward Bound instructor on the *Bowdoin* or the adviser at the MET, for instance, provides the conditions that make students' active exploration of the real world likely, challenging, and fruitful. There is a mutual interchange between the student, the world, and the teacher, but it is the student who most often poses the question and who is the principal agent of his own learning.

Thus, the nature of the work the teacher does is quite different from that in the Transmission of Knowledge model. Some call teachers facilitators of learning. As Outward Bound describes it, "Learning by doing is the style of all our courses. Instructors begin by leading activities and teaching you what you need to know. Gradually, instructors turn the responsibility over to you." Clearly there is a place for the Transmission of Knowledge model, for sit 'n' git, but it does not dominate instruction.

The two models can and do work in complementary ways. A teacher might, for example, give each fourth grader a battery, a piece of wire, and a light bulb. There is a science curriculum here, but the teacher does not *need* to pose a problem, present facts, or direct instruction. Given these materials, no fourth grader (or adult) I have ever observed has had difficulty crafting a question. The questions emerge from the interaction of the student and these pieces of the real world. For one student the question is, "How can I light the bulb?" For another, "I wonder how many batteries it will take to burn out the bulb?" For another, "I wonder if I can make a pretty necklace out of wire and bulbs?" Skillful teachers can help each student explore his or her question, articulate learnings, and share them with others in the class.

A difficulty with this Experiential model, and a reason few teachers and schools turn the tuning knob and explore this different station, is that experiences, unlike worksheets, are seldom uniform. They vary from horse stable to aquarium, from student to student. Even more problematic, the Experiential model of learning is very difficult to evaluate in conventional ways. Who gets the A? The student who lit the bulb, burned out the bulb, or made a necklace with it? What if five students worked together (as they will often choose to do) to construct more complicated circuits. How will *they* be evaluated? What do you test? How do you test it? Other means, such as qualitative descriptive comments, exhibitions, and portfolios, must replace numbers.

The tension between the Transmission of Knowledge and Experiential models, not new, is beautifully depicted in this story that a colleague sent to me:

> On June 17, 1744, the commissioners from Maryland and Virginia negotiated a treaty with the Indians of the Six Nations at Lancaster, Pennsylvania. The Indians were invited to send boys to William and Mary College. The next day they declined the offer:
>
> "We know that you highly esteem the type of learning taught in those colleges, and that the maintenance of our young men, while with you, would be very expensive to you. We are convinced that you mean to do us Good by your Proposal; and we thank you heartily. But you, who are wise must know that different Nations have different Conceptions of things and you will therefore not take it amiss, if our Ideas of this kind of Education happen not to be the same as yours. We have had some Experience in it. Several

> of our young People were formerly brought up at the Colleges of the Northern Provinces; they were instructed in all of your Sciences; but when they came back to us, they were bad runners, ignorant of every means of living in the woods—not fit for Hunters, Warriors, nor counselors, they were totally good for nothing.
>
> "We are, however, not the less oblig'd by your kind offer, tho' we decline accepting it; and to show our grateful Sense of it, if the Gentlemen of Virginia will send us a Dozen of their Sons, we will take Care of their Educations, instruct them in all we know, and make Men of them."

We still have much to learn from our Native American forefathers. And we may be starting to learn it.

A recent article in the *Review of Educational Research*[2] examined ninety-six reviews of adventure education programs from around the world. Students were transported out of the classroom and into the out-of-doors, as the Indians of the Six Nations suggested, and given an opportunity to master river rapids or hike up fourteen-thousand-foot mountains or sail for twenty-eight days to a destination in open pulling boats.

The authors found that students who participate in adventure programs show significant improvement in their problem-solving abilities, leadership skills, social skills, and independence. Overall, the researchers found the gains students made on forty different outcomes, ranging from leadership to improved self-concept, comparable to the gains made through more traditional educational means (in other words, formal education in schools).

But one key finding that surprised the researchers was that the gains of students enrolled in adventure education programs continued to be realized *after* the experience—sometimes months after participants completed the twenty- to twenty-six-day programs. That is, these students continued to learn and develop and show improvement in these many important skills subsequent to their wilderness experience. This type of program contrasts with most

educational programs where, as we have seen, the learning and the gains fade after the program ends, and the books are burned and the class notes filed in the attic. Creating lifelong learners, indeed.

The researchers offered several hunches about this difference in long-term effects: students in adventure-learning programs are completely immersed in their experiences in ways students in schools, taking many courses at once, can never be. Adventure programs set high and difficult goals for students, and they structure tasks so that the students can attain these goals; students receive more feedback on their progress as learners than they do in regular classrooms. Students make decisions and must live with the immediate consequences of their decisions—such as the occupants of an improperly pitched tent getting drenched in the rain. Knowledge earned is better than knowledge learned—if it don't come too dear! The researchers conclude that "research on adventure programs can provide many insights which might inform regular educational contexts." It can indeed, if only we turn that tuning knob.

I believe it is possible to create a school culture that is hospitable to human learning if we turn the tuning knob to stations that invite students and adults to take risks with a safety net, engage in novel and surprising experiences, enjoy a sense of adventure and purposefulness, share leadership with others, pose and solve problems for themselves, find the joy and freedom that comes with hard work, assume responsibility not only for their own lives but for the lives of others, and make a contribution to others.

In sum, learning can be informative or transformative—sometimes both. For example, recently a friend taught me how to take a document from my word processing program and incorporate it into an e-mail message. Voila! My life will never again be the same. In a school that is information rich and experience poor, the learning experiences of students will be only "informative" at best, and usually for only a short period of time. It is impossible to create community or lifelong learners by relying on the Transmission of

Knowledge model 85 percent of the time. In environments or schools that are experience rich as well as information rich, learning is often transformative—and therefore lasting. Transformative learning, as in the case of my daughters on the *Bowdoin*, brings with it a basic change in thinking and behavior that becomes embedded in a person's very being. And it all comes when we risk losing sight of the shore.

6

CRAFT KNOWLEDGE

We know so much more than we think we do.
—*Middle school teacher*

They still tell the story in Maine about a dairy farmer who lived in a modest, even shabby little farmhouse. But before him lay a breathtaking view of rolling hills, grazing cows, silos, hay bales, and lush fields. To make ends meet, the farmer sold off a few adjoining acres as a house lot to a physicist from a reputable university (which shall remain unnamed) in Cambridge, Massachusetts.

The physicist had constructed there a very tidy, very elegant—very anal—little house, which stood in marked contrast to that of his neighbor. Every shingle and blade of grass was in order. The distinguishing feature of the new home was a huge plate glass window overlooking the lovely meadow. One afternoon the physicist was out surveying a small grove of white pine trees that stood between his window and the view. He went up to the largest of these trees and proceeded to go through a little dance: he held a plumb line up to it; he measured the girth; he took out a protractor and measured the angle to the top of the tree and plugged numbers into his hand calculator; he held up an anemometer and recorded the wind velocity.

Then he went inside his tidy house and returned carrying a shiny cardboard box—from which he ceremoniously withdrew a brand new yellow chainsaw. He addressed the large tree again and proceeded to cut into it an impressive notch. Then he felled the tree—right *through* that plate glass window! Whereupon the dairy farmer was heard to exclaim, with only a slightly concealed sense of ridicule, "Now thet's *booklernin' fa' yah.*"

As one who has generated a few books, I have to believe that there is much to learn from writing and reading them. They have their place. But sometimes you can study about it, read about it, hear about it, even watch others do it. But when it comes right down to it, you learn how to cut down a tree by cutting down a lot of trees.

Legitimate Learning

Schools define learning in a limiting, circumscribed, and debilitating manner. "Legitimate" learning in schools occurs when a student sits at a desk, receives instruction from the teacher, participates in discussions led by the teacher, fills out worksheets of problems devised by the teacher, writes papers required and graded by the teacher, and takes tests, usually constructed and corrected by the teacher. If *this* is what learning is all about, small wonder students burn their books and drop out as learners as soon as they get the chance. It's all spinach. Where's the rest of the menu?

So how else might we think about learning? Consider Molly, an eight-year-old girl diagnosed with so-called learning disabilities, who frequently bikes the dirt road in front of my farmhouse. One day the chain came off her new bike. Instead of going to Mom or Dad or the bike shop to get it fixed, she decided she was going to get that chain back on by herself!

She studied the incapacitated bicycle and devised a plan: if she could loosen the rear axle and slide it forward, the chain would fit back on. Then she could slide the axle back again and tighten it up. So she assembled some tools: crescent wrench, pliers, screwdriver. (As her neighbor-"teacher," my part in all this was to offer her my toolbox.) She tried out her idea; she got the chain back on the sprocket, tightened the axle back up, and biked off, exhilarated.

Was that "legitimate" learning? Did she pose a problem for herself that she cared about? Did she analyze the problem, develop a hypothesis about remedying it, and assemble appropriate resources? Did she take action and attain a desired result? Was there evidence of success in her work? Of course.

For us ever to attain the goal of creating lifelong learners, our educational institutions must recognize the importance and power of learning that emanates from the rich range of daily experiences youngsters encounter (and with which we can provide them) and to recognize the intense, personal meaning these experiences have for students. And only when we succeed in relating the curriculum to what is relevant in youngsters' experiences will we begin to "teach" them.

An Inch Wide and a Mile Deep

Students are not the only ones who can learn and continue to learn from their experiences. Teachers and administrators also have their experiences, their bicycle chains. Some in their classrooms, some elsewhere in the school, some outside school. As a student, for instance, each teacher has experienced long, 185-day school years, from kindergarten through college. Each has had the experience of being an aspiring teacher, a beginning teacher, a more experienced teacher. This vast collection of experience constitutes a unique, deep, thick ethnography. $N = 1$, perhaps, but in many settings, for many years.

One would think that fruits from this lifetime of "research" by the participant-observers in the educational enterprise might constitute a treasure trove of knowledge for the practitioner, the profession, and for school reform. One cannot sit in a classroom for sixteen years without learning *something* about a successful—and unsuccessful—learning environment. Nor can one turn the desk around and teach for sixteen years without learning something about teaching and learning. Sadly, our profession seems neither to trust nor to rely on the accumulated wisdom of its own practitioners.

The knowledge base for reforming schools is thought to reside in large-scale social science research—in booklernin'. When policymakers in Sacramento, Tallahassee, or Washington want to know what is right or wrong with public schools, what should be changed, and how school personnel should accomplish these changes, they turn to the work of a Ron Edmonds or a John Goodlad.

Social science research tends to be a mile wide (perhaps based on visits to twenty-five hundred classrooms) but only an inch deep (perhaps an hour in each classroom). There is, of course, also much valuable ethnographic, qualitative research in our profession, but this is not where policymakers turn when they want "world-class standards."

Another knowledge base of inestimable value to the improvement of schools lies elsewhere. This "literature" is much less evident in discussions about school reform than is formal research. *Craft knowledge* is the massive collection of experiences and learnings that those who live and work under the roof of the schoolhouse inevitably accrue during their careers. These are the hard-won insights garnered by teachers, principals, guidance counselors, librarians, school secretaries, and parents about such important educational matters as parent involvement, staff development, curriculum development, discipline, teaching, leadership—and school improvement. By virtue of their experience, practitioners know a *lot* about these matters: for instance, how to teach tenth-grade trigonometry without ability groups, how to "include" in the fourth grade a youngster with severe ADD, how to conduct a successful parent conference, how to talk in a helpful way with students about race, how to conduct a successful teacher evaluation. These are but a few examples of our craft knowledge. We know more than we think we do, indeed!

This knowledge base, unlike the social science research, tends to be only an inch wide but a mile deep. In her entire career, a teacher may have worked in only two or three schools, a small *n* to be sure. Yet she has worked there eight hours a day for 186 days a year for thirty-four years. Tragically, outsiders in universities, legislative committees, state departments, or even central offices rarely view the wisdom from the craft as legitimate or rigorous, let alone as useful to the important work of school reform. Even more tragically, this craft knowledge is rarely viewed by school people *themselves* as legitimate, rigorous, or useful.

The Gold and the Gravel

There are many reasons for the undervaluing of craft knowledge by school practitioners. One has to do with the difficulty of distinguishing the gold from the gravel. When a fourth-grade teacher or a high school principal speaks, it is believed that out will come not craft knowledge but a *war story:* "Let me tell you about the time I tried to involve some parents in developing a new social studies curriculum." Eyes glaze over. War stories are descriptions of practice, verbal portraits of the events of the schoolhouse. I actually rather like telling war stories and listening to others tell them. As a principal, I used to assemble with a few colleagues late on Friday afternoons to drink beer and tell lies. Telling our war stories was therapeutic, we found, a way of cleansing the experiences of the week from our lives so we could go home and begin a restorative weekend with our families.

Craft knowledge, in contrast, is something much more than the telling of war stories. It is a description of practice accompanied by an intentional *analysis* of practice: "Let me tell you about the time I tried to involve parents in developing a new social studies curriculum—and here's what I learned from it." "If I were to do it again, here's how I would do it differently." "Here's what worked; here's what didn't." These hard-won learnings are the gold nuggets we mine from the gravel of our experience.

Another reason that craft knowledge is not commonly valued and exchanged has to do with the tendency within our profession to hoard the gold. I remember, as principal, getting hammered every spring when it came time to assign youngsters to teachers' classes for the following year. Everyone cared passionately about every decision. The sending teacher, the receiving teacher, the student, the parents of the student—and the principal. For over a month, I reeled, I didn't sleep, I was tormented. I thought of moving to Maine and growing potatoes. Yet when I met with the other twenty-three principals in my district, none of them seemed to be having any trouble at all with the placement of youngsters. What were they doing that I wasn't doing? I never knew. We shared our war stories, perhaps. But seldom did we share the craft knowledge that lay hidden beneath the surface of these stories.

A belief commonly held by many who work in schools is that one's knowledge, skills, and successes are a private matter, best kept behind closed doors. This secrecy is amplified by the reality that, in the cruel world of schools, practitioners are placed in the position of being competitors for scarce recognition and resources. "If I tell you how I place children, more parents will want their children in your school than mine, and mine might close down." "If I give you my keys to the store about managing youngsters with ADD, more parents and students will want you than me as a teacher, and my standing and recognition will diminish by comparison." So we educators keep craft knowledge to ourselves, lest others get the few crumbs available on education's table and we go hungry.

There is still another reason why the exchange of craft knowledge is not common in our profession. Even if a teacher or principal chooses to share her craft knowledge with others, it is often not safe for her to do so. The teacher who stands up in a faculty meeting and offers, "I've got this great idea about grouping youngsters in math," violates a taboo that exists within many school cultures: Thou shalt not distinguish thyself from the rest—nor even *appear* to distinguish thyself from the rest. Teachers who share their successes, their learning from experience—teachers who violate this taboo—are likely to be harshly put down by the others. "Big deal; I've been doing that for twenty years." "What's she after, a promotion?"

Recently I attended a celebration honoring the newly designated Milken Award winners. On the basis of their distinguished work as educators, several teachers and a principal were given unrestricted $25,000 grants. As is the case with the McArthur "genius" grants, these educators did not apply for this honor; they were sought out. All the recipients with whom I talked were thrilled by the honor. However, each reported that the one downside of their financial windfall and statewide recognition was that with the receipt of these grants came the disapprobation of many of their colleagues. By being anointed as "distinguished," these Milken Award winners had violated the taboo. They had raised themselves above the rest—and now they were paying for it. This disheartened the award winners, who had expected their fellows to be cheering for their success. Instead, those who did not receive awards appeared to be saying, "If you get this award and recognition for being an outstanding educator, what does that say about *me*, who didn't get it?"

Finally, to be interested in what others have learned about their craft, to learn from them a new or better practice, feeds into the widespread belief and reality that any improvement of practice will be accompanied by an additional, unwanted demand on time and energy. The more and better you perform, the more work you will have to do. Beginning teachers often do share their craft knowledge and seek out the craft knowledge of others. Perhaps they don't know any better, yet. But the school's culture will have its way with them, and thus, over time, it becomes less and less likely that older, more experienced teachers will share *their* craft knowledge, seek it from others, and learn from it. It's easier to keep it to oneself and have others keep it to themselves.

The Wisdom of Experience

New educators coming into our profession as teachers and principals bring with them great powers as observers. They bring new energy, ideas, and hope, and a deep capacity for learning. But it is the veterans and those who are *exiting* the profession who carry with them an abundance of craft knowledge.

Next June, in almost every school in the nation, teachers and administrators will retire, leave the profession forever. And when they walk out the schoolhouse door for the final time, they will carry with them an enormous collection of experiences, and learnings from those experiences. They will be loaded to the gunwale with craft knowledge—which, henceforth, will be forever lost to the school, to their colleagues, and to the profession. In this way, craft knowledge is continually bled off from our schools, taken to the grave—unappreciated, unwelcome, unrevealed, and unused. What a tragic loss to the profession, to the professionals, and to the cause of school reform.

The wisdom of the elders in other societies is respected, sought out, even revered. In North America, for instance, the culture of the Native Americans and Inuits is transmitted from one generation to the next by tribal elders who freely disclose their lifetime of learning. In our society, it's usually "What do all those old fogies know, anyway?"

The magnitude of the loss to our profession from not sharing our craft knowledge is suggested by the magnitude of the gain to another profession from sharing its craft knowledge. A headline in the newspaper read, "Heart By-Pass Death Rate Drops 25% When Surgeons Share Know-How."[1] The article mentioned the following information:

> Twenty-three practicing surgeons and their staffs in three New England states observed one another in the operating room and shared their know-how.
>
> "We didn't invent anything new; we got better at doing the things we already do," said one surgeon.
>
> Seventy-four patients who were expected to die did not.
>
> Outside experts who praised the work said it will be hard to get other doctors to change.
>
> Researchers believe the methods could be applied in other fields.

I wonder how many *children's* lives might be saved if we educators disclose what we know to others.

Celebrating Craft Knowledge

Our profession appears to value neither the giving nor the receiving of craft knowledge. So it behooves us to ask, Under what conditions are educators likely to come to reflect on and to consolidate their craft knowledge, disclose it to others, and put it to work for the purpose of reforming the school, thereby contributing to the formation of a community of lifelong learners?

There are many schools where much is made of the craft knowledge of the teachers and administrators. The Professional Development Schools, the Coalition of Essential Schools, and the League of Professional Schools in Georgia, for instance, are all committed to developing and refining craft knowledge and making it available to others through writing, conversation, and reciprocal visits.

The Galloway School in Atlanta offers a heartening example. There, the faculty and administration have created the Galloway Academy, which is run by teachers. The academy operates on the premise that teachers teaching teachers is the highest form of professional development. Every Thursday morning, it is the practice in the school to hold an open meeting for the faculty, during which any teacher may describe a workshop, seminar, class, or any other form of learning he has encountered that he believes others might like to hear about. More important, Thursday morning is a time when teachers share, in depth, a program or a project or an instructional approach they have developed in response to an important problem or possibility. The meetings begin at 7:30 A.M. and go for about forty-five minutes. Sometimes ideas are picked up, and a group of interested teachers reconvenes at a later time to explore the issue in more detail. The academy, after three years, is considered by the faculty to be a very important part of the school's culture. "That's the way we do things here!"

And then there is storytelling. Recently I've been working with groups of teachers and administrators, encouraging them to tell stories to a partner about their school experiences—about teaching, leadership, parent involvement, unexpected events with children. Then, with the help of the partner, they analyze the story and tease out the craft knowledge and express it as an important learning. By telling their stories to colleagues, practitioners come to reflect on their school experiences, analyze them, clarify them, and elevate the war stories to the realm of craft knowledge. Embedded in every story is an important learning—if we can find it. These workshops convince me that we are one another's best teachers; by telling and listening to stories, together we make sense of the world around us.

Many years ago Rabbi Nachman observed, "God so loved stories that he created man." I find that everyone is a potential storyteller. Storytelling may come easier to some than to others, but there is no teacher or principal, for instance, who does not carry around abundant experiences that are waiting to be told as stories to others. Our lives are made up of them. As part of the repertoire of important ways to promote the recognition and disclosure of craft knowledge, storytelling deserves a prominent place.

For, as Terry Deal puts it, "Without story . . . there is no public dream. Without shared dreams, organizations falter and perish. . . . Leaders must venture off the known and protected pathway to find their own private storehouse. Stories help them choose a direction and learn from their experiences."[2]

Muted Voices

When we value craft knowledge, we develop a school culture hospitable to learning. A central part of the work of the school-based reformer is to find ways to honor, reveal, exchange, and celebrate the craft knowledge that resides in every schoolhouse. The most distressing and infuriating discovery from my "required reading" after the back surgery was that in these vast sedimentary deposits of knowledge about school reform, the voices of school people expressing what they know about good schools and about making schools good were absent. I can think of no other profession in which the voices of its own members are mute in discussions about its reform.

I'm not arguing that the social science literature should be rejected or replaced by craft knowledge. Or that we should abandon booklernin'. I'm arguing that, as yet, school practitioners are not even fielding a team! What is desperately needed in deliberations about the reform of our nation's schools is a continual conversation between social science research and craft knowledge—and between social scientist and educator. Each has tough and important questions to ask the other. I believe that only with the provocation, with the checks and balances each part of the knowledge base provides the other, can we accomplish what neither can accomplish alone.[3]

One thing is sure: if we expect academics and policymakers to value what school people learn from experience in the schoolhouse—our craft knowledge—we first must take ourselves seriously and value our own craft knowledge. When school people come to believe in themselves as leaders as well as learners, as reformers as well as those to be reformed—when they create within the schoolhouse a culture of continual experimentation and invention—others will come to believe in them too.

7

REFLECTION

> Experience is not so much what happens to us as
> what we make of what happens to us.
>
> —*Aldous Huxley*

How do we make something of what happens to us in schools? Over the years, a teacher or principal can have the same experience a hundred times, be it a perplexing budget or a difficult child, and learn little from it. Learning from experience is not inevitable. It must be intentional. Acknowledging, celebrating, and exchanging craft knowledge are powerful means of building a school culture hospitable to human learning. But how do we forge craft knowledge from experience?

A precondition for generating craft knowledge is that we must *reflect* on practice and find meaning in it. It is through reflection that we distill, clarify, and articulate our craft knowledge.

I find the life of a school person akin to that of a tennis shoe in a laundry dryer—congested, convoluted, lumpy, dark, endless. These are not conditions hospitable for contemplation, for finding meaning, for learning. Reflection is precisely the capacity to distance oneself from the highly routinized, depleting, sometimes meaning*less* activities in which we are engaged, so that we can see what's really going on.

So, given our frenetic lives, how can we school people learn to overcome the impediments to reflection that so characterize the school day? How does one become a reflective practitioner?

There is a useful distinction between reflecting *in* practice and reflecting *on* practice. Reflecting in practice is reflecting while one is in the laundry dryer, immersed in the workplace; reflecting on practice is done outside the laundry dryer: at home writing a journal, in a university course, or in a staff development workshop. Clearly, setting has an influence on reflection.

There are a number of ways I see educators reflecting both in and on practice.

Observation

To reflect on practice we must observe practice. As Marcel Proust has written, "The real art of discovery consists not in finding new lands, but in seeing with new eyes." We educators spend much time looking for new lands—new programs, new conceptions of schools from various reformers. Perhaps we might find more satisfaction seeing our own schools with new eyes.

One teacher, in a lovely piece of reflective writing, put it this way: "How long has it been since we visited our own school? Maybe all of us who are interested in restructuring our school should take a long walk down its corridors once more." Another teacher, wishing to become an observer in her school, told this story: "One day I donned a dress I had never worn to school, I drove my husband's car to work, took a different route, deliberately parked in a different part of the lot, and entered through a different door. By the time I arrived inside the school, it had become a different place, one I was able to see afresh, more through the eyes of an observer than of a participant. I spent that day and many subsequent days seeing a *different* school from the one in which I had taught for sixteen years."

Like this teacher, all of us need to invent mechanisms that enable us, in the midst of depleting routinization and overwhelming, unrelenting demands, to get outside the laundry dryer of school life and learn to observe our schools afresh. My favorite philosopher, Yogi Berra, put it this way: "Sometimes you can observe a whole lot by just watching."

Writing

I have a little sign over my desk that reads, "In order to know what I think I have to write and see what I say." When one writes, one thinks, one necessarily reflects. Writing can take many forms, such as journal writing, free writing, memo writing.

I remember that as a teacher, then as principal, whenever something especially noteworthy or satisfying or problematic occurred in the classroom or the school—a particularly successful meeting, a remarkable change in a child, a heated letter from a parent, a sudden insight from a teacher—I jotted it down on the back of an envelope or on a napkin and added it to a pile forming in the bottom drawer of my desk. A few years later, I took a year's leave of absence, looked in my bottom drawer, and found a far different literature than the sedimentary deposits of studies accumulating on *top* of the desk! I assembled these hundreds of bits and scraps of writing into a book, *Run School Run*. Without this record of ideas and insights and anecdotes, I would never have been able to create the book. For without these notes there would have been little memory of the rich details of my school experience. Thus, from my momentary reflections *in* practice, I was later able to reflect more contemplatively *on* practice.

For most of us, writing comes with great difficulty. Yet part of what it means to be a professional is to learn how to write about practice and to disclose one's thoughts in writing to others. When we write we become responsible for our words and ultimately we become more thoughtful human beings. Writing (and reading) about practice is closely related to improving practice, for with written words come the innermost secrets of schools and of their schoolmasters.

Time, of course, is a huge impediment to writing. No school person I know has any discretionary time for this kind of "add-on." The complexity of the subject matter is another obstacle. How does one convert into organized, linear prose the massive, simultaneous onslaught of incidents, behaviors, and feelings that bombard educators each day? Yet when we make a bit of time here and there and develop some meaning-making lenses through which to observe and write about our practice, we find ourselves reflecting on practice, clarifying practice, and learning from practice.

Computers and e-mail now make it easy to share and distribute our little writings, insights, or problems to others. Several years ago, my friend Phil, then a principal in Illinois, invited me to engage in an unusual pen pal correspondence. He would write to me and share what was on his mind about matters educational. His rules: no attention is to be paid to grammar, usage, or correct punctuation—just content; if you have time or want to respond, do; if you don't, then that's fine, too. Phil and I still continue this wonderful form of reflecting together about schools. It demands little and yields a great deal. Often it's easier and more fun to have a friend rather than yourself as your audience. Fortunately, potential educational pen pals abound.

Writing about our experiences in schools is one way to ensure that we reflect on and learn from experience. By writing about practice, each of us comes to know more about what we do and about what we know. Because the written word has a shelf life that the spoken word does not enjoy, those who write about their lives in schools discover that other members of the school community are highly interested in their ideas. Presenting a "hard copy" of our observations and reflections on the subject of, say, school leadership to the interested, critical, discerning eyes of teachers, parents, administrators, and students—risky, to be sure—ensures an ongoing conversation about school leadership in hallways, parking lots, and faculty and PTA meetings. Writing about the school's nondiscussables makes it likely they will be discussed and reflected on. The pen still wields power.

Conversation

Conversations have the capacity to promote reflection, to create and exchange craft knowledge, and to help improve the organization. Schools, I'm afraid, deal more in meetings—in talking at

and being talked at—than in conversation. So how do we transform talk, meetings, agendas, and posturing into conversation?

I like the term *critical friend*, now common in our profession. Each of us needs trusted colleagues who have not only teaching and leadership ability but also human interpersonal skills. Conversations with them can take place in practice, in the schoolhouse, or, as mine with Phil, outside the schoolhouse.

As principal of an elementary school, I met every Wednesday from noon to two o'clock with three critical friends: two teachers (the primary grade leader and the intermediate grade leader) and the school psychologist. Our Wednesday get-togethers were sacrosanct. We religiously maintained our commitment to them for six years. Our agreement was simple: to show up on time and stay the full two hours (no small commitment for a teacher, psychologist, or principal); to bring to the conversation issues and problems about the school we wanted to discuss; to honor the issues and problems the others wanted to discuss; and to keep our conversations confidential. No agenda was presented. We just showed up and talked. Sometimes we talked to resolution or to decision. Occasionally we made some very inspired decisions. Sometimes we just talked. But always we tried to be honest and respectful.

It is no surprise that each of us looked forward to these conversations. They were as much about relationships as about issues. Sometimes they were contentious, but the honesty was refreshing, the views of others novel, and the collegiality authentic. Furthermore, each of us drew sustenance from these conversations, both from unlimbering and from being listened to. We found that reflecting about school practice by oneself beforehand and to others during the conversation offered great survival strength. In short, our conversations caused us to be reflective. Reflective practitioners can stand at a distance from a difficult environment and see it for what it is—and isn't. They are less likely to be overwhelmed or overcome by it, and more able to improve their school.

The power of conversation in the business culture is described by Juanita Brown and David Issacs, two consultants whose findings are remarkably similar to what we experienced in the Wednesday meetings.

> All of us have, at one time or another, experienced a conversation that has had a powerful impact on us—one that sparked a new insight or helped us see a problem in a radically different light. What sets apart this type of generative, transformative conversation from the many exchanges that occur on a daily basis at our workplaces and in our homes? What are the qualities that make it worthwhile?
>
> We have posed this question to hundreds of executives and employees. Common themes include:
>
> There was a sense of mutual respect between us.
>
> We took the time to really talk together and reflect about what we each thought was important.
>
> We listened to each other, even if there were differences.
>
> I was accepted and not judged by the others in the conversation.
>
> The conversation helped strengthen our relationship.
>
> We explored questions that mattered.
>
> We developed shared meaning that wasn't there when we began.
>
> I learned something new or important.
>
> It strengthened our mutual commitment.

Most relevant to our discussion here was the authors' conclusion that "knowledge creation is primarily a social rather than an individual process."[1]

Maybe we educators *can* learn from business! Our Wednesday conversations and these reports from business suggest that it might be prudent occasionally to reverse the expectations of schools: from "Stop talking and get to work" to "Stop working and get to talk!" Or, even better, to "*Start* talking and get to work!" Conversation is an essential ingredient of our work.

How do we change the climate of fear, mistrust, and hierarchical control that so stifles honest conversation? We will need to set up some ground rules (like those from my Wednesday meetings), create physical environments that encourage knowledge-generating shared conversations, and accord precious time worthy of this precious activity. With authentic conversation comes reflection on practice and thus improvement of practice. Conversation then becomes a powerful instrument of school reform—and a kind of inquiry to be taken very seriously.

Embracing Differences

The existence of differences and how they are received is also highly related to a culture of reflection within the school. In schools where every teacher is using the same reading series, everything is smooth; few questions are asked, and there is little reflection about how we teach reading here. But in a school where one teacher is using a formal reading series, another across the hall is using an individualized program, and a third is teaching reading through youngsters' daily experiences, teachers necessarily reflect. Teachers are aware of, and constantly examine, what others are doing and the results they are finding. Therefore, they reflect on what *they* are doing and the results *they* are finding. All these teachers have much to reflect on, just as a school that has African American, Asian, white, and Hispanic youngsters has much more to reflect on and bring to a discussion of race than a school composed of all white or all black youngsters. There is much wisdom in the old adage that says we find comfort among those who agree with us—and growth among those who do not.

Differences often bring with them unevenness, expense, tensions, even conflict. But the objective of our work as educators is not to create a dissonance-free environment but rather to create a learning-full environment, to build a community of learners. I choose unevenness, tension, even conflict for what they may bring to reflection and learning, over homogeneity and calm accompanied by less reflection and therefore less learning.

As I reflect on my years as an elementary school teacher and principal, it seems my greatest difficulties and most abiding satisfactions have been associated with the tension between uniformity and diversity. Underlying most of the day-to-day problems, decisions, and conflicts I recall so vividly is a fundamental question: On what occasions must all teachers and all children in a school behave in the same way, and when is it acceptable—even desirable—for them to differ?

This tension is evident in the current press for high standards and in the preoccupation with "high-stakes" standardized tests. The greater the influence of standardized tests on a school, the greater the likelihood that the instructional program, the faculty, and the school will become uniform. There may be much truth in the words on a wonderful T-shirt I saw in the parking lot of a high school: "High Stakes Are for Tomatoes."

Tomatoes notwithstanding, uniformity among teachers and their classrooms, instructional styles, curricula, programs, and means of evaluation conveys the reassuring appearance that the school has found the one best way to teach everything and everybody. Uniformity makes school boards, superintendents, curriculum coordinators, parents, and even children feel secure that we educators know what we're doing.

The existence of differences, in contrast, often suggests uneven quality and performance. And differences can lead to friction and conflict. Our society is experiencing a rise in hate crimes; special interest groups are proliferating; immigration policies are under attack. Sometimes it appears that the dream of our American culture as a melting pot is melting down.

At the school level, if everyone on the faculty is doing the same thing in the same way, teachers may get along. But if they do things differently, "Whose arithmetic program is the best?" and "Which teacher is the best?" are always in the air. Competition, insecurity, and tension are heightened. Sometimes there are meltdowns.

Yet differences *abound* in schools, whether we like them or not. There are differences among students and teachers in terms of social class, gender, race, age, ability, and interests. There are difference in roles of students, teachers, and principals. And there are differences in learning styles and teaching styles.

I find that schools handle differences in several ways. Some deny them. Differences simply don't exist. As in "By June, all students will . . ." As in, "It really doesn't matter into which sixth-grade class we place Johnny; all the teachers are the same and teach the same thing the same way."

Other schools accept differences—but as a painful fact of life. Each teacher is assigned and has to deal with a certain number of low-achieving children. Each principal must deal with that errant, troublesome teacher.

And many schools recognize differences and then attempt to group them out: fast students here, slow there; college bound here, vocational there; boys here, girls there. All, of course, "in the best interests of the youngsters." Differences bring problems.

Still other schools find it impossible to deny or group out differences and end up constantly embattled over them: the teachers' union versus the administration; the black gang versus the white gang; the jocks versus the nerds; the school people versus the central office.

Only a few schools work hard to attend to, acknowledge, honor, and celebrate differences, because they believe pronounced differences are often accompanied by pronounced learning. These schools are committed to the question, How can we make conscious, deliberate use of differences in social class, gender, age, ability, race, and interests as resources for learning? They believe that what is important about human beings is what is different, not what is the same. In such schools, authenticity abounds.

So do reflection and learning. When we were starting the first Summer Institute at the Harvard Principals' Center in the early 1980s, we sought seventy-five participants. Twice that many applied. A problem of success. But which seventy-five to admit? The best and the brightest? Those with good references and test scores? Refreshingly, the team of principals leading the institute decided that we would admit the seventy-five *most different* principals we could find. Only then, they argued, would learning curves go off the chart. And they did. And still do.

When you put twelve principals from the same district around a table talking about, for instance, parent involvement, the discussion is limited. However, when you gather in conversation about parent involvement a dozen principals, one from a three-thousand-pupil New York City high school, another a K–12 teaching principal from a tiny Inuit school on an island off the coast of Alaska, another from a wealthy suburb of Philadelphia, and others from similarly discrepant settings, reflection and learning about parents are inevitable. Such groups of individuals who differ are ever so much more vibrant, interesting, and strong than those whose members are homogenized. E pluribus unum!

Diversity is abundant and free. Its presence prompts comparison, observation, and examination of "the way I do it." Used wisely, deliberately, and constructively, it offers an untapped, renewable resource available as fodder for reflection in every public school. We should learn to use it well. Pluralism rather than uniformity, eclecticism rather than orthodoxy—these offer our greatest hope for building a community of learners and a culture of lifelong learning. Fortunately, people come to school that way—different.

• • •

John Dewey once defined reflection as "a specialized form of thinking, arising from perplexity about a direct experience and leading to purposeful inquiry and problem resolution." If reflecting on practice can help our profession move from perplexity around direct experience toward problem resolution—and if it can help us come in touch with our craft knowledge—it has much to offer to school reform and to school reformers.

Personal reflection on our experience is *how* we learn from experience. Reflection contributes to the refinement of subsequent action and to the building of a repertoire of professional craft knowledge. And, of course, reflecting on practice—by observing practice, by writing about practice, by engaging in conversation about practice, by embracing the differences we encounter in practice—builds a school culture hospitable to both learning and community.

8

TEACHER LEADERSHIP

> A community is like a ship; everyone ought to be prepared to take the helm.
>
> —*Henrik Ibsen*

To this point, we have been considering a vision of a good school for youngsters and adults, which I have called a community of learners. This is a school that has succeeded in creating a culture hospitable to human learning. In addition, the school culture fosters in students and adults a disposition toward independent, insatiable, lifelong learning. Such a learning environment is characterized by, among other things, experiential learning, abundant sharing of craft knowledge, reflection, observation, writing, conversation, and embracing differences.

Lofty ideas. But how to "walk the talk"? How to move, in the real world, toward such an ambitious vision? That is, how to put it all into practice?

Now I would like to tell some stories about teacher leadership that embody these ideas. These are stories not about transforming youngsters' learning experiences but about transforming those of adults. I believe that the first step in reforming the learning experiences of young people is to reform the learning experiences of the adults responsible for young people's education. For as Albert Schweitzer once said, "Example is not the main thing in influencing others. It's the *only* thing."

To the extent that in their own learning, school people have experienced stations on that radio dial different from sit 'n' git; to the extent they have found satisfaction, learned in new ways, been transformed by those experiences, and become lifelong learners—to that extent I believe these educators will now have the ability, the desire, and the heart to transform the learning experiences of their students in similar ways. You can lead where you have gone!

Teacher Leadership at Sea

An adventure is an experience whose outcome one does not know in advance. Allow me to tell an adventure story.

I once helped put together an activity on shared leadership and decision making for a group of educators. We enlisted the sturdy sailing schooner *Bowdoin*, the same vessel on which my family had sailed from Rockland, Maine, to Gloucester, Massachusetts. On this passage, a far different cast of characters assembled. Teams consisting of teachers, principals, and superintendents representing school districts from throughout Massachusetts shipped aboard for the day.

While the vessel was tied to the dock, the Outward Bound crew demonstrated how to get the many sails up and the anchor down, where the charts were stowed, and how to read the compass and run the engine. The sit 'n' git attended to, we then sailed out into Boston Harbor and abruptly dropped both sails and anchor. Our mission for the day, we were instructed, was to sail the schooner back to the Charlestown Navy Yard by 4 P.M. Then, to our amazement, the crew went below into the cabin, and the experiential learning began!

How does a group of sixty people, largely unacquainted, possessing abundant egos and varied backgrounds, get organized and fulfill a very complex task? Who does what? Who leads? Who follows? Who watches? Meanwhile, tugboats blasted, destroyers powered close by, recreational vessels buzzed around us, and all the while jet liners, landing at Logan Airport, skimmed over the masts of the *Bowdoin*. The pressure was on. The stakes were high. The boatload of educators was on the line. Rather like a school!

After a prolonged period of what could only be described as chaos, the suggestion was offered by a teacher that we might take inventory of who on board remembered any of our dockside instructions. Had anyone been listening? (Sometimes we *need* the information from sit 'n' git!) Could anyone recall, for instance, in what order the five sails were to be raised? Was the anchor to be raised before or after the sails? (Five percent recall from our brief lecture would have been a generous estimate!) Next we took inventory of our collective sailing experiences. Did anyone know how to read a nautical chart? Could anyone relate the chart to the compass and actually navigate? Was anyone familiar with the "rules of the road" with respect to other vessels? And so it went. After an hour or so, chaos slowly began to give way to some heady and hearty conversation, even collaboration.

As it turned out, an elementary school teacher was teaching a unit on map and chart reading; a high school teacher raced sailing dinghies and was well acquainted with right of way. Another teacher had recently been on a windjammer and had taken several turns at the helm.

So, as most of the principals and central office officials stood by, observed, and received orders, the teachers took over. The sails were raised, then the anchor. And a small band of public school teachers, providing clear leadership and deft seamanship, brought the *Bowdoin* and its occupants safely back into the dock at the Charlestown Navy Yard. It was 4 P.M.

Our little band of educators then spent the next five hours in groups, reflecting on our passage and what we had learned from it about shared leadership in schools. We were becoming a community of learners! We talked about whether it was rank that denoted special expertise in, say, navigation, or whether it was prior experience, or having listened during the instructions and being able to remember, or possessing the personal authority to be taken seriously. Well into the dark hours, the cabin brightened by the glow of the ship's kerosene lantern, we considered how our experience sailing the *Bowdoin* back into port resembled the work we do in schools to promote youngsters' learning. Finally, before we set out for home, we brainstormed, in light of our day on Boston Harbor, how each team would now go about its work.

One incontrovertible learning from the day was that you don't have to be or to become a principal or a superintendent in order to influence the course of a vessel—or a school. Indeed, rank in the hierarchy has little relevance when it comes to school-based reform. Reformers are those who know something about the organization, have a vision leading to a better way, can enlist others in that vision, and can mine the gold of everyone's craft knowledge to discover ways to move toward that vision. As Frank McCourt, author of *Angela's Ashes* and a former classroom teacher suggests, "Ask the teachers—for a change. They're on the front lines. Forget the bureaucrats and politicians and statisticians. Ask the teachers. They know the daily drama of the classroom, a drama beyond measurement."

There was another learning from that day on the *Bowdoin*. As part of the assessment of teacher productivity in our profession, the group suggested we should ask, Is the real teacher showing up? Is *all* of the teacher showing up as it did on the *Bowdoin*, or is much of it left at home each morning? We are all capable of our best and of our worst. Teachers who give their best most of the time offer schools their leadership. It is in teachers' hands, every bit as much as the hands of the school principal, that possibilities for school-based reform reside.

Indeed, assuming leadership to improve the school, like writing about practice, is part of what it means to be a professional. There is no shortage of opportunities in school for the teacher to demonstrate professionalism by leading, a few tough steps at a time, toward improvement.

With increasing frequency these days, teachers are evaluated on the basis of how successful they are in getting their students' test scores to rise. Perhaps a more fundamental criterion would be to look at how helpful teachers are as members of the school community in providing leadership that will improve the culture of the school and make it hospitable to everyone's learning. For, as we know, more than anything else it is the culture of the school that determines the achievement of teacher and student alike.

Our day at sea aboard the *Bowdoin* vividly manifests the untapped potential and power of teacher leaders, yet the culture of most schools and school systems provides precious little support for teacher leadership. Indeed, as we have discussed, the teacher who steps in and assumes leadership, who distinguishes himself or herself from the others, violates the taboos of many schools and districts.

When teachers' leadership is withheld or rejected, there are incalculable costs to both teacher and school. For without teachers' leadership, all too few vessels get their sails up and their anchor raised, and make it safely into port. And the life of the teacher becomes limited to the classroom—a rich and crucial life, to be sure, but not enough for most teachers and most schools.

Benefits of Teacher Leadership

Let's consider further the problematic issue of teacher leadership by considering its possible benefits. Why should some teachers choose to have a positive influence on their schools beyond the classroom? Why is the language of the burgeoning number of charter schools replete with such phrases as *empowerment of teachers*, *faculty participation in management*, *authority of teachers*, and *consensus management?* Something must be in it for somebody. As it turns out, there's a great deal in teacher leadership for everybody.

The Students

One oft-stated fundamental purpose of public education commonly found in curriculum guidelines is "to equip our citizens to believe in and to participate fully in our democratic system." To accomplish this goal, we require students to take courses in civics, social studies, and citizenship. A sobering evaluation of the success of our efforts is found by a look at voter participation at the polls: fewer voters register and vote in this country than in any other Western democracy. Moreover, between 1972 and 1996, voter turnout among high school graduates (eighteen- to twenty-four-year-olds) in presidential elections fell 20 percent to just 32 percent.[1] Clearly, not many students are graduating from our schools really believing in, let alone practicing, democracy.

Few schools operate democratically. Their governance is more akin to a dictatorship (albeit usually a benevolent one) than to a New England town meeting. I know. I used to be a benevolent dictator principal. I used to think that I shared leadership with teachers. And I did. Rather, I should say that I went as far as I could go or felt the school could go. But reflecting years later on my leadership, I see that shared leadership for me was delegating to others, giving away to others, or sharing with others the making of important decisions—as long as the curriculum, pupil achievement, staff development, and, of course, *my* leadership were not much threatened. I also used to be the faculty adviser to the student council. When a student initiative went beyond keeping the school playground clean or installing larger lockers, I would rule it out of order on behalf of the faculty and administration. Through such daily lessons, through what we teach in what is often called the hidden curriculum, we succeed in conveying to students that democracy is a fraud.

If few students experience their school environment as democratic, the same goes for teachers. In contrast, when teachers take on important schoolwide responsibilities and are encouraged and supported in such efforts, they take a huge step in transforming their school from dictatorship to democracy. This change in the leadership culture of the school is not lost on students. Ripple effects soon radiate throughout the building as teachers enlist student leadership to amplify their own. And the more the school comes to look, act, and feel like a democracy, the more students come to believe in, practice, and sustain our democratic form of government.

Students win in other ways. Studies of governance patterns in high-performing schools—that is, those with few discipline problems and high pupil achievement—suggest that decision making and leadership are significantly more democratic. The teachers are more involved and influential in establishing discipline, selecting text books, designing curriculum, and even choosing their colleagues than are teachers in low-performing schools. What can we take from these kinds of studies? That students learn when teachers lead!

The School

A school culture hospitable to widespread leadership will be a school culture hospitable to widespread learning. School cultures promote and celebrate continual learning for students only when teachers join the community of lifelong learners. In order to create communities of learners, teachers must model for students the most important enterprise of the schoolhouse—learning. A teacher who has stopped learning cannot create a classroom climate rich in learning for students. Yet the dominant structure of a school—the repetition of classes, a reliance on textbooks and workbooks, someone else dictating what a teacher should do—is not one that can promote and sustain profound levels of adult learning. Indeed, as we have seen, learning curves turn downward. If their teacher is not a learner, students soon recognize that the message is "Do as we say, not as we do."

Our work in schools is to get learning curves off the chart—upwards. A powerful relationship exists between learning and leading. The most salient learning for most of us comes when we don't know how to do it, when we want to know how to do it, and when our responsibility for doing it will affect the lives of many others with whom we live and work. This is where teacher leadership and professional development intersect.

Teachers who assume responsibility for something about which they care desperately—a new pupil evaluation system, revising the science curriculum, or setting up a computer lab—stand at the gate of profound learning. The way to learn is by leading; the way to lead is by learning. Teacher leadership provides an inevitable and continual occasion for teacher growth. The teacher who is always leading and learning will generate students who are capable of both leading and learning.

Pogo observes that none of us is as smart as all of us. When decision making is dispersed and when many minds are brought to bear on the knotty, recurring problems of the schoolhouse, better decisions get made about curriculum, professional development, faculty meetings, scheduling, and discipline. The better the quality of the decisions, the better the school.

The more educators are a part of the decision making, the greater their morale, participation, and commitment in carrying out the goals of the school. Imagine a school where *every* teacher takes ownership for a portion of the entire organization! When many lead, the school wins.

The Teachers

Most would agree that who the teacher is and what the teacher does in the classroom have a greater influence on students' accomplishment than any other school factor. There is considerable evidence, also, that what the teacher does inside the classroom is directly related to what the teacher does outside the classroom. The lives of teachers who lead are enriched and ennobled in many significant ways. Rather than remain passive recipients, even victims, of what their institutions deal to them, teachers who lead help shape their schools and, thereby, shape their own destinies as educators.

It may seem curious, once again, but a good place to look for successful examples of teacher leadership is within universities. Major decisions in universities are made through byzantine routes that involve various hierarchies within the priesthood. But when you get right down to it, at most universities the *faculty* outranks the administration and reigns supreme.

At Harvard, for instance, members of the senior faculty of the Graduate School of Education make decisions about hiring new faculty, recommend to the president names of those who should receive tenure, are deeply involved in the decision to hire a dean, provide oversight on the budget, and make key decisions about new degree programs. Clearly these teachers influence the course of the vessel.

Few public school faculties ever approach this level of teacher leadership in matters of program, budget, and personnel. But why not? Higher education drives in so many ways what goes on in K–12 schools; why not in matters of teacher leadership? Furthermore, if teachers are going to be held more and more accountable for student achievement, shouldn't teachers enjoy more and more authority for determining how the school will function?

Happily, many examples of teacher leadership in K–12 schools exist. Take, for example, the efforts of the faculty at City on a Hill Charter School in Boston. They have taken seriously their commitment to systemic change of urban public schools by launching a teacher's institute within the school. The purpose of the institute is to continually invigorate the school's faculty and to serve as a site for the preparation of new urban teachers. Teachers like these enjoy many advantages:

The teacher who leads gets to sit at the table with grown-ups as a first-class citizen in the schoolhouse rather than remain a subordinate in a world full of superordinates.

The teacher who leads enjoys variety, even relief, from the relentless tedium of the classroom. An abundance of worthy, very different educational challenges awaits every teacher beyond the walls of the classroom.

The teacher who leads has an opportunity to work with and influence the lives of adults, as well as those of youngsters.

These are among the benefits for the teacher who teaches *and* leads. The teacher leader has much to give and much to gain. Empowerment, community service, recognition, parity, and stimulating variety are indeed benefits of consequence.

The Principal

If there ever was a time when, like John Wayne or Joan of Arc, the principal could save a troubled school by riding in alone on a white horse, those days are certainly over. The myriad complexities and demands of the job are well known. I know of no administrator who doesn't need and want help in fulfilling this impossible job description. Parents, students, community members, universities, business partners, the central office—all have the potential to become wonderful resources and allies for the principal. But the most reliable, useful, proximate, and professional help resides under the roof of the schoolhouse: the teaching staff itself.

When teachers pull an oar for the entire school by setting up a computer lab or developing a new science curriculum, they offer valuable assistance to the overworked and overwhelmed principal and to the school itself. Ample evidence suggests that effective principals don't work harder than less effective principals—they work smarter. Principals who encourage and enlist teachers' leadership leverage their own.

All Teachers Can Lead

Schools badly need the leadership of teachers if they are to improve. Teachers become more active learners in an environment where they are leaders. When teachers lead, principals extend their own capacity, students learn and live in a democratic community of learners, and schools benefit from better decisions. This is why the promise of widespread teacher leadership in our schools is so compelling for the success of school reform.

I would like to put forth the revolutionary idea that all teachers can lead. Let me take the notion one step further: if schools are going to become places where all children and adults are learning in worthy ways, all teachers *must* lead. Skeptics might amend this assertion to "some teachers" or "a few teachers" or even "many teachers." These low expectations are as destructive and as likely to lead to limiting, self-fulfilling prophecies as the idea that only some children can learn. Schools suffer from an overabundance of underutilized talent. The fact of the matter is that all teachers harbor extraordinary leadership capabilities waiting to be unlocked and engaged for the good of the school.

I envision a school that is a community of leaders. This is a place whose very mission is to ensure that every student, parent, teacher, and principal will become a school leader in some ways and at some times. All are in the same boat and, as Ibsen says, ought to be prepared to take the helm. Leadership is making happen what you believe in. Everyone deserves an opportunity for school leadership. Schools can help all the adults and youngsters within their walls learn how to earn and enjoy the recognition, satisfaction, and influence that come from serving the common good. And we can all learn in schools to accept the helpful leadership of others. It's exciting to speculate about what would happen if, in addition to becoming a community of learners, every school were to become such a community of leaders.

All teachers have leadership potential. The world will come to accept that all teachers can lead, as many people now accept that all children can learn, if educators can overcome the many impediments that block teachers from leading and can provide conditions that make it likely that teachers will exercise leadership.

To extend this discussion, I would like to share in Chapter Nine a remarkable experience during which many teacher leaders in the state of Rhode Island taught me that teacher leadership can be an idea every bit as promising as it is perilous.

9

IMPEDIMENTS AND OPPORTUNITIES

> It's hard to care for a class of little bodies and still have time and energy to lead.
>
> —*Rhode Island teacher leader*[1]

"One memorable occasion!" That's how one Rhode Island teacher leader described it.[2] In winter 1998, the Rhode Island Foundation hosted in Providence the gathering of a remarkable group of educators. About one hundred teachers assembled from across the state. Twenty-five were Sizer Fellows, previously awarded grants to explore and develop the rich and problematic relationship between school and home for adolescent students. Another seventy-five teachers were trainers in the foundation's Rhode Island Teachers and Technology Initiative (RITTI), a $5.7 million effort to provide training and laptop computers to more than 25 percent of all public school teachers in the state. In addition to their full-time classroom duties, all these teachers—the Sizer Fellows and the RITTI trainers—have taken on the challenge of improving their schools beyond their classrooms, of becoming leaders in their schools.

We began at four o'clock on a dark December afternoon. The teachers had worked a long day, driven to Providence, and were now facing another four or five hours during which they would be asked to think hard, discuss, listen, and explore the frustrating and elusive topic of teacher leadership. There was no lethargy, however. The room pulsed with that singular energy we experience on those rare occasions when voracious learners challenge the boundaries of understanding. During the course of this meeting, many came to see themselves differently. As one teacher wrote,

> I never looked at myself as a leader. The events of the evening forced me to look at myself and my school in a new light.[3]

When the one hundred Rhode Island teachers at the Providence meeting were invited to "stand up if you're a leader," perhaps two-thirds of them, with evident caution and hesitation, stood up and identified themselves as leaders. I suspect that part of the caution, even reluctance, among these and other teachers to stand as leaders in their schools is related to confusion about the meaning of the words *leadership* and *teacher leadership*.

I once visited an innovative middle school to learn how decisions were made. After engaging a teacher in conversation for a while, I asked her, "Do you take on some leadership for this school?" Clearly, the question struck a raw nerve. "I'm just a teacher. If you want to talk with a leader, he's down the hall in the principal's office." Her response abraded, and continues to abrade, a raw nerve within *me*. More important, this teacher's words identify and aggravate a very sore place in our profession. "I'm just a teacher" indeed!

What is the difference between being just a teacher and being a teacher leader? I think of a teacher leader as one who has a positive influence on the school as well as in the classroom. If we accept this definition, we might identify a number of different activities through which the teacher can influence the well-being of the school. Prominent among them are participating in the creation of a school vision; shaping curriculum for the school; setting standards for student behavior, promotion, and retention; planning and leading staff development activities; engaging in decisions about how funds shall be allocated; and hiring new teachers and administrators.

These are among the conditions of schooling that affect a teacher's ability to work with students; they are the domains in which teacher leadership is most needed and least seen.

Each of us, I suspect, has a different conception of what we mean by teacher leadership. As I have said, I think of teacher leadership as the act of having a positive influence on the school as well as in the classroom. I also like the economy of the definition offered by one of the Rhode Island teachers:

> Initiatives by teachers which improve schools and learning.[4]

To be sure, some teachers enjoy a corrosive influence by subverting. Others are "yes, but" people. I am convinced, however, that all teachers have the capacity to lead the enterprise down a more positive path, to bring their abundant experience and wisdom to schools. But I wonder how many principals and other administrators believe it? More important, do teachers believe it?

One of the Rhode Island teachers captured the essence, perhaps, of the entire gathering in Providence when he came to regard himself, maybe for the first time, as a teacher leader:

> It feels great to be appreciated. I get a lot of energizing from being called a leader in education. I feel honored to be considered a leader in education for my contributions to improve the use of technology in the classrooms.[5]

The voices you will hear in this chapter were recorded at the small-group sessions that evening in Providence. In addition, each teacher participant was invited to subsequently offer written comments about the obstacles and opportunities teachers face when they try to exert leadership in schools. From this highly charged gathering of inventive teacher leaders emerged some strong prose, thoughtful reflection, and considerable craft knowledge about the impediments to teacher leadership they have experienced—and about the conditions that can overcome those impediments.

Impediments

It is evident that the concept of teacher leadership holds great potential for building community, promoting learning, and enriching schools and the lives of principals, students, and teachers themselves. The idea is compelling. Why, then, do so few teachers contribute so little to the life of their schools beyond their classrooms? Why do teachers hesitate to stand when asked if they are leaders in their school? If teacher leadership is such a good idea, why isn't everyone doing it?

There are reasons. Good ones. Many of them. They boiled to the surface with remarkable clarity and energy, and occasionally with anger, at the conversation in Providence. It is all very well to cite the virtues of teacher leadership; regrettably, severe, crippling impediments stand in the way of realizing this dream. What teachers have to say about the barriers to teacher leadership is important for our profession to hear.

Our Plate Is Full

> Recently the only thing about our school that the majority of faculty members could come to consensus on was that our plate is full.[6]

Some of the conditions within the school culture that thwart teacher leadership come as no surprise. Responsibility upon responsibility has been added to each teacher's working day: responding to parents, overseeing after-school activities, attending professional development activities, and, of course, maintaining standards. The list is staggering. As a teacher once told me, "When was the last time someone said to me, 'Sandra, you are no longer responsible for . . .'? It's always an add-on."

In this context, the "opportunity" for chairing a school site council, setting up a computer lab, or taking charge of a staff development day can feel like an unwanted portion on an already too-full plate. The fact of the matter is, most teachers are overwhelmed with existing duties. School leadership is an add-on, a desirable add-on perhaps, but an add-on nonetheless. When choices must be made, many teachers understandably choose to teach, not lead.

There's Never Enough Time

> An obstacle I face is that there never seems to be enough time to get together in my building to talk and share ideas.[7]

> For systemic change to occur, colleagues need time, quality time to work together.[8]

It *is* all about time. Time is *why* the plate is full. Time in schools is in finite supply and in infinite demand. For most, it is a question of living within the allotted twenty-four hours in a day. How many teachers have been heard to say, "I would love to chair the committee, but I don't have time"? For most it is the truth. There simply is not enough time to do it all, let alone do it all well.

Others feel they have or could make time, but they expect to be paid for it. Some unions don't look kindly at teachers who take on additional leadership functions without pay. These unions set and enforce limits on teachers' allocation of uncompensated time and draw attention to those who breach the limits. Many teachers find they can exert more power by saying no than by saying yes. And why not? Endless uncompensated add-ons eventually lead to the schoolhouse equivalent of a sweatshop.

> [Our] union uses restraints of the contract to convince teachers to follow time limits in their work in schools. Doing "extra" jobs (jobs that are unpaid or not in the contract) that are often the very work that can improve student learning is discouraged.[9]

Teachers lead demanding lives outside of school. Three-quarters of teachers nationwide are women, many of whom bear major responsibility for their own children. Others are fathers, spouses, or caretakers of elderly parents. Still others hold outside jobs to make ends meet.

Time is indeed precious. The plate *is* full. Most of the work of the teacher leader *is* uncompensated. Thus, it is not difficult to understand why a majority of teachers confine themselves within their classrooms, resolved to the work that is important for compliance and to the work that they believe is right for their students.

All of this leaves unexplained the puzzling paradox that those teachers who seem to have the least time and the most on their plates are the very ones who always seem ready and able to take on the additional work of schoolwide leadership. Like most principals, I soon discovered that if something had to get done, I needed to find a "busy person" to do it.

Tests Rule

> Administrators, school committee members, teachers, and indeed, the entire "system" itself—we are all being held hostage by the test scores.[10]

The current preoccupation with accountability and standards has been widely translated into standardization, tests, and scores. Increasingly, the feeling in schools is that everything must be sacrificed on the altar of the standardized test. Accountability is ratcheted up and up by constant, comparative scrutiny of the scores by teacher, by grade level, by school, by district, by state, and by nation. The public, it seems, will have its pound of flesh, which will come in the form of improved performance by students on standardized tests.

Standardized tests are having a chilling effect on the teaching profession and on the inclination and ability of teachers to assume broad leadership in their schools. Every moment of every teacher's day is being scrutinized to discover what change might raise a student's scores.

It is virtually impossible, of course, to link a teacher's leadership of a professional development day with salutary effects on the achievement level of that teacher's students. "What's my responsibility for such a day got to do with raising my students' scores to the 85th percentile?" has become a common, debilitating question.

The answer in the short run, demonstrably, is "very little." So the teacher, mindful of what the system does and does not value and reward, chooses not to take responsibility for shaping the professional development day. The tyranny of the tests rules the day, every part of the day. And like a tyrant, this obsession with tests and scores has invaded aspects of schooling that go far beyond the content of a student's class. It is possible that the test scores will rise, but at costs that unfortunately will not be factored into the equation. The discussion has gone so far off track that the unquestionably valuable concept of standards has been divorced from all that goes into building the kind of school culture that leads naturally to the attainment of those standards. I wonder if these tests have an iatrogenic effect. That is, does the attempt to remediate a problem cause a greater problem than the one we were originally trying to solve?

Withstanding Opposition from Colleagues

The Rhode Island teacher leaders were resolute in their belief, refined over years in the crucible of the schoolhouse, that full plates, time crunches, and standardized tests are not the only or even the most severe barriers they face when sailing into the uncharted and dangerous shoals of school leadership. Their greatest concern was reserved for far more critical and influential elements in their schools: their colleagues. If they can get by the Sirens of time, tests, and tight budgets, their reward is the Scylla and Charybdis of fellow teachers and administrators, who wield an immense power to extinguish a teacher's involvement in school leadership.

> It is sad, but sometimes we are our own worst enemies.[11]

A teacher in another state once told me, "We have gathered our wagons into a circle and trained our guns—on each other."

The reports of the Rhode Island teachers, similar to what I hear from teachers elsewhere, suggest various school climates surrounding teacher leadership; they range from supportive to indifferent to inhospitable to toxic. Unfortunately, the balance is skewed toward the toxic end of the continuum.

There are many reasons why the teacher who would lead encounters resistance from fellow teachers. Opposition often comes in bizarre, enervating, and discouraging forms. Some are passive—inertia, caution, insecurity, primitive personal and interpersonal skills—others are active.

Inertia. Inertia is endemic in most academic institutions. Principals lead; teachers teach. So it has been and so it shall be.

> The biggest challenge is trying to get to teachers in my building who are set in their ways. There are some teachers who are not willing to listen to new ideas or strategies. The few have made it hard for the rest of us to try new things.[12]

Caution and Insecurity. Coupled with institutional inertia is another quality familiar to many school cultures: aversion to risk. It can be as unsafe to lead as it can be unsafe to follow the lead of another, especially when neither is an officially "designated" leader. In the world of teacher leadership, danger abounds. If sharing craft knowledge is risky for teachers, taking leadership is more so.

And so caution abounds. One of the Sizer Fellows reported that he had given up pursuing his project because it had been dependent on his teaching a certain class, which got scheduled to someone else at the last minute. The more he thought about it, however, the more he found himself asking hard questions about himself:

> Why didn't I go to the superintendent and explain what the schedule change was doing to my work? Why didn't I go to the teacher who got assigned to that class to see whether we might pursue the work together? Why didn't I ask the students if they had any ideas about how we could salvage the project? Instead, I threw up my hands, railing against the "system" when I should have been helping make the "system" work for me.[13]

Each of his possible responses carried risk. From the teacher's startling admission, it was clear that in retrospect, he wished he had taken the risks. To his greater credit, however, he had the courage and will to reflect on and learn from this difficult experience.

Ours is a very cautious profession, top to bottom. Linked with inertia and caution is insecurity. The Rhode Island teachers were outspoken about the prevailing insecurity they experience among many teachers in their schools. As one teacher said,

> When a teacher is truly passionate about her work, others are threatened because they don't feel it, or can't impart it to their students. Sometimes I feel impeded in my work by teachers and administrators who are threatened by my enthusiasm.[14]

A kind of taboo among teachers in many schools makes it difficult to disclose one's excitement to peers. Many teachers don't possess the courage or self-confidence that allows them to violate this taboo.

Primitive Personal and Interpersonal Skills. A final source of passive resistance to the teacher leader, found in many schools, is the primitive quality of the relationships among teachers.

> I really think teachers need to rely on each other for knowledge and an exchange of ideas. Teachers need to build a network of support. We need to be able to communicate.[15]

Many school faculties are congenial, but few would characterize themselves as collegial. The classic hallmarks of collegiality—talking about practice, sharing craft knowledge, rooting for the success of others, observing others in their work—simply are absent. Many teachers seem to lack the personal, interpersonal, and group skills essential to the successful exercise of leadership and to working together. The following story, told by one Rhode Island teacher, suggests the extent of the deficiency.

> Recently, I sat with a group of educators from several different school districts to talk about student reading responses and to share our craft knowledge about what we believe is exemplary student work at the grade level that we teach. I thought that all teachers would love to talk about student work and about classroom practice, so I envisioned a worthwhile conversation with colleagues that I could use. I was completely taken aback at how miserably the morning went. Two teachers sat red-faced and unable to contribute comfortably for at least an hour. One teacher was combative and only wanted to share if the sharing was on her terms. One teacher interrupted others more than once. The majority of the group felt the need to defend why their students did not do as well on this test as they would have liked. I began to share my thoughts on the task, hoping to encourage the group toward open communication about the student work, but realized through reading body language and listening carefully to the contributions of individuals that the group was not going to be comfortable sharing. This task was too risky for a majority of members.[16]

Active Resistance to Teacher Leadership. Inertia, risk aversion, lack of confidence, and primitive adult relationships all thwart teacher initiatives toward school leadership. Collectively, they provide a backdrop on which more active forms of resistance from teachers play out.

> In every school community there are veteran teachers who have "been there, done that." Some are well practiced at sitting back

and waiting for new ideas to die; others act to make sure the ideas die. Whatever the discussion, the first group dismisses most, if not everything, of what is suggested. The second group actively sets up road blocks. Want to reorganize the day? Can't. The contract doesn't allow it. Want to form interdisciplinary teams? Can't.[17]

Colleagues who do not want to be involved in a change idea will sometimes sabotage the efforts of a teacher who is actively pursuing that change.[18]

I asked several teachers to get together once a month after school to share ideas, lessons, and so on. Everyone thought it was a good idea until we tried to set a date. No one could agree on a day because some people had other jobs, children at home, after school clubs, and the like. It was very difficult. When we finally agreed on a date and got together, it turned into a gripe session. Some complained about the discipline, others about administration. Although these are legitimate concerns, it wasn't what this meeting was intended for. I became very frustrated. The once-a-month meeting soon stopped.[19]

Sometimes even the strong support of the principal is insufficient to cushion the teacher leader against the formidable opposition of other teachers. One teacher told the following story:

Our building administrator, as usual, was supportive and encouraged us to take the lead in discussing this topic. We did some research, attended a conference, and spoke with a couple of schools already involved in looping [a teacher remaining with the same group of students for two or more years], and finally brought the topic to a faculty meeting for discussion. We made a presentation to the faculty following this research. The reaction of other teachers, who had been informed and updated about the upcoming discussion, was disappointing and disheartening. Most were silent. Those who did speak were unsupportive, at best. There was an unwillingness even

> to engage in a discussion on a topic which we thought should be, at the very least, of interest to educators. I was disappointed. I was even more disappointed (although not surprised) to learn that there had been a great deal of discussion about the topic in the teachers' room, but that discussion had not been with those of us who were initiating the discussion.[20]

The array of means that teachers persistently, insistently employ to sabotage the best intentions of others is daunting and discouraging. Many teachers are left perplexed by the unfriendliness of their school's culture toward teacher leadership. They have experienced, as one teacher put it, that "leadership can turn to ostracism."

Passive and active resistance by other teachers, when played out on the stage of full plates, insufficient time, lack of compensation, and standardized tests, all but brings the curtain down on teacher leadership. Many teachers are content with trying to become a distinguished leader in their tangible classrooms where they can lead young people in relative safety and with considerably more control and satisfaction. They opt out of being leaders in their schools or within their profession.

Opportunities

Happily, fellow teachers also hold the power to unlock one another's leadership potential and to foster its growth. Far more than workload, time, or tests, the basic disposition of a school toward the value of teacher leadership—the nature of a school's culture, "the way we do things here"—ultimately determines whether and by what means teachers will participate in the school community as leaders.

If leadership is making happen what you believe in, *how* do you make it happen? Teachers believe strongly in many things. If a teacher believes, say, in strengthening parent involvement in the school and wants to make that happen, there are several choices.

As these Rhode Island teachers, disheartened yet undaunted by the impediments, clearly document, there are many ways to lead. These educators reveal a repertoire of hopeful means by which they are having a positive and significant influence on their schools as teacher leaders.

Lead by Following

> Many teachers choose to follow, even though they have the ability to lead.[21]

Perhaps the least risky, demanding, complicated, and therefore most common way to influence the life of one's school beyond the classroom is to follow the lead of others. By selectively supporting the efforts of fellow teachers, one teacher can help others move mountains and occasionally even more massive geological formations, such as schools.

In our American culture, however, it's as difficult to identify oneself as a follower as it is to call oneself a leader. Indeed, most of us were raised in households where being a follower was always cast in a negative light. Of course, it's the way one follows and the leader one chooses to follow, rather than following itself, that determines whether one's decision to follow is strong and principled or weak and pedestrian.

Following the lead of others may seem like a modest contribution on the part of the teacher leader, but it often constitutes a significant, affirmative, even courageous form of leadership and of school-based reform. For anything of consequence to get done in schools, many are needed to contribute in a hundred subtle, periodic, and reliable ways. This can mean showing up and speaking out at an important public meeting, signing petitions, writing letters, and participating in the cheering section. The success of those at the front of the line depends on the support of those behind them. "Followership" is an art form yet to be discovered by many educators and schools. More schools will improve when more teachers turn their considerable energies toward judiciously following others.

Join the Team

Referring to his colleagues who gathered for our meeting in Providence, one educator noted,

> These teachers are team players. They have an ability to bring those around them into the process. Thus begins the process of change. By providing the same support and enthusiasm they bring to the classroom, they build the next step in the process: teams of teachers and students working toward common goals.[22]

Another teacher put it this way:

> If schools are going to be run by a committee, then I want to make damn sure I'm on the committee.[23]

So they join in a collective effort, not as a follower but by sharing leadership with others. Teams and committees offer some safety in numbers for the cautious, companionship for the gregarious, challenge for those attempting to influence others, and greater hope for all of making a significant difference through combined strength. And because more perspectives are considered, teams also often make better decisions than individuals.

When teachers on a team share a common purpose and common ground with each other, they can tolerate frustration with long meetings and disagreements; and as a team member, a teacher often finds it possible to make happen what he believes in. We have all experienced the profound influence of a single member of a team, and we have all seen examples of the extraordinary influence a team can have on a school. This is why many teachers

find greater satisfaction in being a part of a high-performing team than in solitary accomplishment.

Lead Alone

> I plan to continue to do my work in my own quiet way and try to influence as many people as I can by my example.[24]

Because they may be dissatisfied with following the lead of others, and because they experience impatience and frustration trying to work with colleagues as team members, and perhaps having been thwarted or ignored by administrators, many teachers set out alone to influence their schools. Oftentimes they take this course of necessity, only after pursuing "the correct route" without success.

One of the Rhode Island teachers described it this way:

> In the past, I have taken the correct route to try to get things done. I go to the principal and get told no. Then I write a letter to the school committee and the superintendent and get ignored. Then I just go and do it myself. I have decided to just go get it myself. Maybe it's not right, but it gets the job done.[25]

These teachers may conceal their attempts to improve their schools. They become covert, guerrilla warriors. For them it is safer, simpler, faster, and perhaps more exciting to go underground, disclosing what they have done only when success is certain. This way, their efforts do not depend on enlisting the support of others, and they risk no public failure should their project prove unsuccessful. If their effort—at raising money for a school, for example—succeeds, however, the impact of guerrilla leaders is often compromised by the clandestine nature of their work. There is no one to share in the celebration, as there was no one to share in the project. Nevertheless, despite the many impediments faced by teachers who set out to lead alone, a great many find success. If we define the teacher leader as one who has a positive influence upon the entire school, as well as in the classroom, even the teacher who goes it alone—without followers, team, or visibility—can lead.

Lead by Example

Very different from their guerrilla cousins, solitary teacher leaders who stay out in the open are more likely to have a positive influence on the larger school community, because they take the risk to provide a constant, visible model of excellent practice as well as of persistence, hope, and enthusiasm. By their example, they influence others.

> The best teachers I have known have shown leadership by holding out their excitement for teaching like a beacon and by keeping it focused on student welfare. Their model inspires other teachers. It also brings other teachers along with them in their zeal.[26]

And indeed, I have seen stunning examples of teachers offering leadership to their school by remaining within their classroom. They bring others *in*—to observe their work, to reflect, to have conversations, to tell stories, and to exchange their craft knowledge about teaching. Teacher leader, indeed.

Leading by example is perhaps the purest form of leadership and the one over which each of us has the most control. You can lead only where you will go.

What It Takes

The Rhode Island teachers suggest that success of teacher leaders is related to three factors:

1. *Have a goal.* Teachers who can identify and clearly delimit a goal—who care passionately about and can convincingly articulate the change they want to see in the school—are likely to ex-

perience some success, especially if they recognize how others might benefit from that change.

> I had a goal to try to get a scanner purchased for my school. I decided to create a school Web page so my principal could see the benefit of it. She loved it and has agreed to make the purchase for the scanner, a color printer, and a digital camera. I will be running a faculty workshop on how to use this new equipment.[27]

2. *Persist.* Teachers who succeed in influencing the school are tireless, incessant, and undeterred by the obstacles that seem to leap from behind every bush. Commitment to their cause is stronger than the hurdles they encounter.

> Tenacity, persistence, and handling rejection well are admirable qualities of a teacher leader.[28]

> I have learned that persistence generally pays off. Obstacles should never be seen as insurmountable. Defeat can only happen with capitulation. I suppose that Don Quixote may be an imperfect role model, but he has his qualities.[29]

3. *Define success as incremental.* Tilting at windmills can be a dangerous activity, especially if one gets so tangled in the dream that satisfaction can come only with total fulfillment. The real world of schools seldom allows total fulfillment of anyone's dreams.

> When we built our first weather station, many teachers came to me and said it wouldn't last and that the kids would trash it. It hurt, but I was stubborn and felt it was worth a shot. It took quite a while to train my students in the proper way to take measurements, much longer than I had anticipated. Then it was time to start transmitting data.
>
> Unfortunately, the teachers who thought it would never work were right: the station was trashed. We picked up the pieces and rebuilt the station again, only to have it trashed over the summer.

> The following fall we rebuilt it for the third time, only to find that our phone line was pulled because the school was installing a 56K line in the building. While I was trying to decide if I could handle transmitting the data from home, the station was destroyed for the final time. It was hard listening to the "I told you so's," but it was still worth the effort.
>
> The GLOBE computer is constantly in use in my classroom, and the activities I learned have found a place in my curriculum even if my students and I could not participate in the project the way I wanted to. I've even shared some of the activities at workshops, so the whole experience was not a total loss.
>
> It was not my most successful project, but I learned that it was OK to try new things. I don't like to fail, but I did learn from the failure.[30]

Teachers who define success as an increment of change in the desirable direction, rather than as accomplishing everything they set out to, experience success, feel "it was still worth the effort," and are likely to engage in subsequent initiatives.

• • •

When it comes to changing a school, these then are among the options and strategies available to every teacher: lead by following, join the team, lead alone, and lead by example. Some teachers may see these as deliberate, intentional choices; others select by default. Some may go with one choice this time, another the next. Each approach offers different advantages and disadvantages to the teacher and to the school.

But the bottom line is that teachers become school-based reformers only when they take on leadership for important parts of the school that lie beyond their classrooms. Or they lead by bringing important parts of the school into their classrooms. Either way, by taking the risk to lead, they help construct within the school a community of leaders. A school that is a community of leaders will always be engaged in self-renewal.

10

TEACHERS AND PRINCIPALS

> The true measure of a leader is not how many followers you begat, but how many leaders you begat. —*Ralph Nader*

I once attended a PTA meeting at which, in describing her innovative school, the principal slipped (I think!) and remarked, "At Riverside Elementary School we live on the bleeding edge."

As a teacher and then as principal, I learned over and over again that the relationship among the adults in the schoolhouse has more impact on the quality and the character of the school—and on the accomplishment of youngsters—than any other factor. Put differently, when the alarm rings at six in the morning, the alacrity with which a teacher jumps out of bed depends upon which adults that teacher will encounter that day and around what contentious issues. Unfortunately, because of the primitive quality of adult relationships in so many schools, all too few teachers respond with enthusiasm to that alarm. The bleeding edge is not a good place to work.

Among adult relationships in schools, that between teacher and principal is decisive. I have found no characteristic of a good school more pervasive than healthy teacher-principal relationships—and no characteristic of a troubled school more common than troubled, embattled, or antiseptic administrator-teacher relationships. The relationship between teacher and principal seems to have an extraordinary amplifying effect. For better or for worse, it models what *all* relationships in the school will be.

It follows, then, that the teacher-principal relationship is at the heart of shared leadership in schools. The nature and quality of this relationship is absolutely central to the capacity of a school to become a community of learners—and leaders. So what shall it be? Superordinate to subordinate? Adversarial? Supportive? Collegial? Cooperative? Clearly there is nothing inherent in the role of principal that causes either curtailment or support of teacher leadership: what matters is how the principal chooses to perform the job. Through their day-to-day actions, principals build the culture of their schools. That pattern of behavior can embed teacher leadership in the school's culture, cast a wet blanket on such leadership—or have no influence at all.

Leaders influence through *positional* authority, which comes with the job description, and they influence through *personal* authority, which they earn by who they are and how they conduct themselves. One way many teachers become leaders in their schools is by leaving the classroom and assuming positions as assistant principals and principals. They acquire positional authority. Yet many teachers who want to offer leadership in their schools do not want to become a principal or even to be *like* a principal.

I wonder if principals are aware of how often they present to teachers an image of school leadership as something undesirable, if not reprehensible. By their example, how many principals discourage teachers who would be principals or teacher leaders? Several Rhode Island teachers expressed a disturbingly negative perception of the role of the school principal:

> I think many talented individuals remain in the shadows because they hear colleagues talk about administration in a negative way.[1]

> Unfortunately, the job of a school administrator has become one that seems to have less and less to do with educational issues and more and more to do with managerial issues. I have no interest in being involved in this aspect of education.[2]

> I will never be a principal because I would be losing the one thing that makes every day of my life a pleasure: going to my class.[3]

Rightly or wrongly, teachers seem to link their perception of the principalship to leadership in general. The logic seems to follow these lines: "To be a leader is to be like an administrator. I don't like the plight of administrators. I want none of it for myself. Therefore, I will stay away from teacher leadership."

A healthy, productive learning community should not have so many of its most valuable citizens recoiling at the thought of assuming the top leadership role in that community. Teachers might not want the position of principal, but how much better if they see it as something they respect and admire and something that symbolizes the best the profession and the school has to offer.

A teacher may sometimes choose to exercise leadership independently, but few initiatives to improve a school may be undertaken with disregard for the school principal. Administrators have a disproportionate influence on the teacher who would be a leader—for better or for worse.

The Rhode Island teachers are crystal clear in expressing the importance of the school principal, not only in leading a school but in creating an environment that encourages—or discourages—others to lead as well.

> Some administrators embrace the energy of staff members to join in leadership roles, and provide much support for people who want to take the lead. They show support for grant writing or support for organizing a group to work on an idea. The positive power of administrators and teachers working together to improve schools is awesome.[4]

Indeed! Their influence together is far greater than when either is going it alone. If teacher leadership is critical to the health and performance of a school, principals are crucial to the health and performance of teacher leaders.

Let's consider more specifically how principals exert a negative or a positive impact on the development of a culture of teacher leadership.

Principals as Barriers

It is disheartening that so many teachers experience their school administrator, and especially their principal, as an obstacle to their leadership aspirations. They see principals holding tightly and jealously to power, control, and the center stage.

> Leadership from any other sphere often causes a negative reaction unless, of course, the idea comes from the administration and the leadership is appointed by the administrator.[5]

There are good reasons why principals guard their authority. They have worked long and hard to get where they are. First as classroom teachers, then through countless nights, weekends, and summers in exhausting administrative preparation programs, then through an arduous job search. Now that they have secured a position as leader of the school, they protect it tenaciously as their special province.

And, just as it is risky for a teacher to assume leadership, it is risky for a principal to share leadership with teachers. Because principals will be held accountable for what others do, it is natural that they want evidence in advance that those empowered will get the job done well. Principals also are mindful of how much care, feeding, and hand holding must go into helping the teacher leader. Why set up and tend a committee to hire that new teacher? Given their own time crunch, many principals find it easier to make decisions themselves.

For all these reasons, many principals carefully control whether and to whom they bestow responsibility for important decisions. They offer leadership opportunities to teachers most likely to support the principal's agenda and who will not divert attention or energy by pursuing their own. As one teacher said,

> The administrator's task is to influence a chosen few and have these teachers, indirectly, advocate his position on issues.[6]

But a pattern of repeatedly anointing the chosen few overloads the few while squelching the leadership potential of the unchosen many. A principal's attempts to control also give rise to that guerrilla teacher leader, who, because she will never be invited by the principal to lead, *must* work surreptitiously.

Although they may not be aware of it, many principals transmit to their staffs forbidding, unwelcoming messages about teacher leadership.

> Part of me feels that administrators do not want to hear the voice of the teacher.[7]

A principal's disposition to share leadership with teachers (or others) appears related to personal security. Many of us have observed that the weaker the principal is personally, the less the principal is likely to share leadership. Stronger, more secure principals are more likely to share leadership. It makes sense. It's as if teachers and principals must learn a new dance together. In order not to step on each other's toes, each must learn some new steps, new rhythms, perhaps new music.

Principals as Culture Builders

So what can the principal do to help teachers reconcile their crucial classroom work with equally crucial schoolwide responsibilities? How might more teachers be sustained rather than discouraged in their efforts to lead?

Other principals who preside over precisely the same kind of schools and who work under an identical job description find ways not only to encourage but also to inspire a culture of teacher leadership in their schools. "That's the way we do things here." Happily, the stories of the Rhode Island teachers are replete with examples of these effective principals.

> The school administration has been most supportive when I have initiated any type of leadership within the school. This support has been of various types: time has been provided to meet with others, to attend conferences, and to otherwise investigate issues; money has been provided when needed. Most important, administrators have encouraged and supported the type of risk-taking that is involved in teacher leadership.[8]

Just what do principals do that has such a powerful influence on the development of teacher leaders? They support. But what exactly does *support* mean? Several factors seem to influence the success of these principals in creating a culture of teacher leadership.

Expect

Principals who support teacher leadership really believe in it and articulate this as a central purpose of the school. The participation of teachers as leaders is much more likely to occur when the principal openly and frequently articulates this vision at meetings, in conversations, in newsletters, in memos to the faculty, and at community meetings. "Teacher leadership is not only welcome here, it is *expected*."

Deborah Meier, the principal at the Mission Hill Elementary School in Boston, says, "A school is a community. By virtue of the fact that teachers are citizens of that community, I expect each of them to take responsibility in some way for the well-being of the school. That's what members of a community do."[9]

High expectations have been associated with academic achievement of youngsters. We are beginning to believe that all children can learn. Similarly, when principals expect teachers to become committed and responsible school leaders, they instill the equally lofty message that all teachers can lead. And all teachers do lead.

Relinquish

In their bottom drawer, principals have a few marbles of authority that came with the job and many more they have earned over the years. Some principals play these marbles alone. Others don't play them at all, making few decisions and allowing others to make fewer. Principals who support teacher leadership make sure that all the marbles are played by as many players as possible. Principals have learned that when they relinquish some of the marbles to teachers, they unlock and enlist the latent creative powers of the faculty in the service of the school.

Entrust

Teachers will not become leaders in the school community if the principal violates teachers' trust, disempowers them, and reasserts authority the minute the going gets rough and an angry parent or central office official makes a phone call. It takes only a single incident of having the rug pulled from beneath a teacher leader before that teacher—and the entire faculty—secedes from the community of leaders.

Empower

When she is confronted with a sudden problem—for example, a reprimand from the fire chief and superintendent after a plodding school evacuation drill—it is common for a principal to set up a new procedure and then recruit a trusted teacher to monitor and maintain it. Yet the fun, the learning, and the commitment around leadership come from brainstorming and devising one's own solutions and then trying to implement them. A principal elicits more leaders and more leadership when she invites teachers to address the problem before, not after, she has determined a solution.

Include

To address a nagging school issue, the principal often selects a trusted teacher who has handled similar problems successfully. But by relying on the tried and proven teacher, the principal rewards competence with even more work. In a short time, the overburdened teacher concludes that his plate is full and retreats to the classroom.

Principals who build a school culture in which teacher leadership can flourish are more likely to match an important school issue with a teacher who feels passionately about that issue. One teacher's passion may be fire safety; another's the computer center. Still another's might be serving as the conduit with the local press, as an able facilitator for discussions among parents, or as the sleuth with a knack for finding new professional development opportunities for colleagues. One person's junk is another's treasure.

Too often, the criterion for bestowing leadership on an individual is evidence that the person knows how to handle the problem. Innovative solutions also come from teachers who don't know how to do something but want to learn. When the teacher is committed to leading, the principal and other faculty members have both an opportunity and a responsibility to help that teacher develop new leadership skills.

When a principal accords opportunities for leadership to untried (and perhaps untrusted) teachers who express passionate interest or concern about an issue, everyone can win. The oft-chosen teacher is overburdened no longer. The teacher, who feels strongly about the issue and is now entrusted with resolving it, comes alive as an adult learner and leader. Rather than being excluded or becoming a guerrilla leader, the teacher joins the community of leaders. And the principal's efforts this year to help induct new teacher leaders will be rewarded next year by less drain on the principal's time and energies, by the sharing of the work of leadership with others who welcome it, and by the recognition that comes to teacher and principal alike for contributing to an improving school.

Protect

As we have seen, teachers who reveal themselves as leaders and thereby distinguish themselves from the others violate a taboo and become "at risk." Principals must find ways to run interference and protect members of the faculty from the assaults of their fellows. A teacher calls a meeting; the principal attends to support and to show the flag. A teacher wants to share at a faculty meeting her craft knowledge about creating a multicultural curriculum; the principal "asks" that teacher to address the faculty. When it's clear to teachers that their leadership is protected, they will exercise it.

Share Responsibility for Failure

If, as inevitably happens, a teacher stumbles in a schoolwide effort, the principal has several options. One is to blame the teacher and absolve himself of the responsibility. This may help the principal in the short run, but in the long run, few teachers will choose to stick their necks out again. Alternatively, the principal can assume the lonely and self-punitive position as captain of the ship: "The ship has gone aground; I am responsible."

But teacher and principal can share responsibility for failure as well as for success. Usually a school community deals more kindly with mistakes made jointly by teacher and principal than with those made by either alone. Of course, the important question is not, Whose fault is it? but rather, What happened, and what can we learn from it so that we do better next time?

When principal and teacher share a foxhole, the outcomes are often collegiality, staff development, safety, trust, and higher morale. Much can be gained from stumbling—together.

Give Recognition

It is as important for principals to share success with teacher leaders as it is for them to share failure. Principals have plenty of opportunities each day to be on center stage, visible to the school community. Teachers have few and need more. The principal who hogs the limelight and deprives teachers of deserved recognition thwarts the development of teacher leaders. Let the teacher bask in the glory of a new, distinguished fire evacuation system or take the credit for helping open a door to a summer fellowship for a colleague. Good principals are more often hero makers than heroes.

I find it ironic that teachers, principals, and parents see clearly the value of student recognition and have assembled an array of ways to offer recognition to students, from gold stars to scholarships, while developing no comparable offerings for the outstanding work of teachers. Recognition of teachers' efforts, including their efforts as leaders, is in precious short supply in the culture of most schools.

Positive recognition comes in many forms: a title like Master Teacher; additional compensation; reduced teaching load; responsibility for a budget; allocation of prime space; an appreciative note from a parent; or acknowledgment by the principal in the school newsletter. Teachers also gain recognition from writing for publication about the work of teacher leadership, from having their craft knowledge respected, or from taking some responsibility for the profession beyond their school. Recognition costs little—sometimes nothing in dollars—but when that alarm rings day after day at 6 A.M., recognition is among the reasons a teacher keeps bounding out of bed with alacrity.

Teachers are telling us, pure and simple: "I will commit and sustain the investment of time, energy, risk-taking, tedious meetings, inconvenience, and intrusion on my classroom and on my personal life. I will pull my oar as a school leader *if* what I do is acknowledged and valued by those around me." Teachers will not for long go through the heroic efforts of leading schools, in addition to teaching classes, if the consequences of their work go unnoticed, unrecognized, or unvalued by others—as one Rhode Island teacher articulated so well:

> I personally think teachers are crying for respect. They want to feel they are valued and productive members of the school community.[10]

Conversations among the Rhode Island teachers give us much to ponder. They suggest a rich repertoire of ideas and practices available to principals who want to beget leaders and thereby demonstrate that schools can *be* democracies as well as teach about them. This is what teachers mean when they say that "support from my principal has been a huge factor in my becoming a teacher leader."

A Preferred Future

Responsibility for creating and sustaining teacher leadership goes beyond the principal in the schoolhouse. To capture the potential of teacher leaders, the profession needs to invent, expand, and honor a variety of opportunities for teacher leadership so that there will be more choices than being "either" a principal or a teacher. The career ladder for teachers has precious few rungs. If more widespread teacher leadership is to be attained in our schools, educators will also have to explore multiple conceptions of the teacher's role: team leader, lead teacher, teacher researcher, master teacher. There is no more important form of "school restructuring." Only when many such roles exist within our profession will the potential to benefit schools that resides in teacher leadership and teachers themselves be realized.

In the next decade, 2.2 million new teachers will be needed to staff America's schools. Approximately two-thirds of the entire teaching profession will be replaced. Thus, the coming decade brings with it a profound opportunity to *re-create* the teaching profession. How would we like it to be?

As the new teachers come into view on the horizon, schools and school systems can post any job description for "teacher" they choose. They can expect of the new arrivals any kind of professional work that offers hope of transforming schools into communities of learners and leaders. These prospective teachers have not yet been inoculated by the prevailing school culture against leaders or against leading. If we choose, as has Debbie Meier, all schools can expect that all teachers *will* lead. The only subject for negotiation need be the manner in which each will take on some important responsibility for the betterment of the entire school community. But first we must transfer teacher leadership from the position it occupies in so many schools—that of being a nondiscussable—to one of being a discussable.

With our nation's schools under relentless scrutiny, with all of the probing and prodding, with all the well-placed concern, a remarkable gap exists for teachers to fill. Most concerned people know what they *don't* want in schools; a smaller number know where the re-forming of schools ought to lead us; and very few know how to get there. There are many right answers, and we are most likely to find them when teachers step into various kinds of leadership roles, share their craft knowledge, and articulate for the public and for the profession just what school and teaching might become.

When teachers lock their cars in the parking lot each morning, too many of them also lock up astonishing skills, interests, abilities, and potential. Then they go inside and teach five classes of beginning algebra and monitor the lunch room. To be sure, teaching algebra is critical to the school, and so is the fulfillment of supervisory duties. Yet an opportunity resides within each of those 2.2 million new teachers, and within the veteran as well, to become far more than "just a teacher" at a school whose only leader resides down the hall in the principal's office. Each of these teachers can become—and must become—a school-based leader and thereby a school-based reformer. For only when we transform and re-create the teaching profession in this way will we be able to transform and re-create the nation's schools.

The Crucial Choice

Teachers face a complex choice about whether they will attempt, in addition to classroom teaching, to influence the entire school. A subtle yet definitive calculus determines the outcome of the decision:

Teachers who choose to confine their work as educators to the classroom *win*. They have more time and energy to devote to their teaching, to each of their students, and to their responsibilities outside of school. They are less susceptible to interpersonal conflicts with other teachers and with the principal. They enjoy a measure of safety in the relatively risk-free sanctuary of the classroom, where they may be accountable for pupil achievement but not for their own achievement as a school leader. And they may enjoy a measure of sanity each day in the often turbulent and chaotic world of the schoolhouse. This is the path the majority of teachers follow.

Other teachers—a smaller number, to be sure—take a different path. In addition to their work as classroom teachers, they choose to expand their contribution to the school by assuming responsibility, some of the time, for some of the issues integral to the health and character of the entire school. By participating in the larger arena, these teachers *lose* what the larger group wins: time, energy, freedom from interpersonal hassle, and immunity from public criticism for efforts that might fail. And they probably lose, as well, a measure of sanity in their days at school and at home.

But the teachers who choose this path *win* more than they lose. Through enhanced companionship and collegiality with other adults, they reduce feelings of isolation; through improving their schools, they experience personal and professional satisfaction; they enjoy a sense of instrumentality, investment, and membership in the wider school community; they experience the new learning about schools, the process of change, and about themselves that accompanies being a leader; and they experience professional invigoration and replenishment, which spill over into their classroom teaching. These teachers become owners and investors in the school, rather than mere tenants.

These are two very different paths taken for very different reasons and with very different implications for the teacher, the school, and the profession. In the past, the majority of teachers have chosen to confine their work as educators to the classroom. Yet the future of public education rests upon a new majority of teachers who will extend their work as educators to the entire school.

11

ON BECOMING A PRINCIPAL

> The way to learn is by leading. The way to lead is by learning. —*Anonymous*

We've all heard it said, "Show me a good school, and I'll show you a good principal!" As the experience with Rhode Island teacher leaders demonstrates so vividly, the school principal exerts an extraordinary influence on creating or thwarting a culture of school leadership. And the principal wields the same capacity to create or thwart most everything else that goes on in a school. Too often this influence is not used fully—or it is abused.

Since the early 1970s when our profession rediscovered the importance of the school principal, policymakers have wrestled with four major implications of that discovery. If the school principal has such an extraordinary influence on the quality of a school, then (1) How do you identify, from many candidates, those likely to become outstanding principals? (2) How do you get these individuals to choose to become principals? (3) Once the aspiring principals have been identified and recruited, how do you prepare them for the crucial—and overwhelming—job they will assume? (4) How do you sustain and extend their learning once they become practicing principals?

In this chapter, I consider the preservice preparation of school principals. In Chapter Twelve, I will consider the continuing professional development of practicing school principals. These chapters are about creating principals who will be visible, sustained, lifelong learners. In our profession, one is a learner and *thereby* a leader. And, as we noted at the outset, only when their important role models embrace learning will students learn.

Alas, the means by which our profession engages in the crucial work of selecting aspiring principals and transforming them into successful practicing school leaders are, at best, questionable. Brian O. Brent, professor at the University of Rochester, summarizes research on the efficacy of the training given aspiring principals. While acknowledging the limitations and paucity of the research in this field, he concludes that "graduate training in educational administration does not positively affect administrator performance." In his review of the literature, Brent finds considerable evidence to support the following points:

> "Principals are generally dissatisfied with their graduate programs, consistently rating their training between poor and fair."
>
> "The more experience principals have, the more dissatisfied they are [with their programs in educational administration]."
>
> "Formal education has no bearing on principal effectiveness."
>
> "Graduate training makes principals less effective."
>
> "There is little evidence that graduate training increases the effectiveness of school administrators in general, and principals, in particular."
>
> "Neither the general level of principals' graduate training nor specific training in educational administration has a positive influence on the measures of school effectiveness."

And there may be little cause for hope about the capacity of the "priests" to reform the priesthood: "Professors of educational administration have a higher regard for the relevance and effectiveness of their administrator preparation programs than do their students."

The central question posed by Brent "is not whether aspiring principals require training beyond classroom teaching experience to be effective leaders. But, why should we expect that graduate school is the most effective place to receive this training?"[1]

My own anecdotal "research" reveals similar findings. When I ask distinguished principals, "So, how did you come to be such an accomplished school leader?" at the bottom of almost everyone's list I find "formal coursework in universities"—lectures, papers, and exams. At the top of almost everyone's list appears, "I learned from experience, by spending a lot of time in schools with an outstanding mentor who was accessible and interested in my development." If we believe what these principals tell us, then it is important to reexamine educational administration programs, which commonly require students to spend about 90 percent of their time with formal course work and perhaps 10 percent in schools with mentors and experiences. And it is even more important that we find better ways to prepare school principals.

The Aspiring Principals' Program

I would like to share the story of a promising new preservice preparation program for aspiring school principals. The Aspiring Principals' Program (APP) addresses, in a holistic way, all the policy questions surrounding the career development of school principals: recruitment, selection, preservice, and in-service professional development. The program, based on the Experiential model of learning, manifests most of the major ideas presented in the preceding pages. APP participants create a culture hospitable to human learning; take part in a community of learners that is both information rich and experience rich; play different stations by celebrating and making full use of their experiences and differences as valued sources of knowledge; and pose their own questions and address them by enlisting their powers of reflection, conversation, writing, and storytelling. In short, as we shall see, the Aspiring Principals' Program translates many of the foregoing ideas to concrete practice.

There is a story behind the creation of the Aspiring Principals' Program. Dennis Littky and Elliot Washor were coprincipals of the Metropolitan Center (MET), a small, innovative, public secondary school in Providence, Rhode Island. Formerly, they enjoyed together some turbulent years at Thayer High School in Winchester, New Hampshire. Jay Casbon, a former principal, is dean of the graduate school of education at Lewis and Clark College in Portland, Oregon. Lewis and Clark, along with Northeastern University and Johnson and Wales University, now provide the academic umbrella and principal certification for the APP. I came into the conversation at Dennis's invitation.

For several days one winter, the four of us sequestered ourselves in the living room of Dennis's modest nineteenth-century tradesman's house near the Providence docks. We took turns at the rocker, the couch, and the straight-backed chairs assembled around a little table. We munched candy bars and nachos, drank cider and soda—all the while provoking one another to dream about what we want our schools to be like in the new century and how to develop leaders for them. Farrell Allen, the observer and scribe, took notes. In short, we engaged in conversation—as educator Elliot Eisner puts it, that "kind of inquiry to be taken very seriously."

Learning Through Experience

Each of the four of us values and trusts the educative powers of experience. We value and trust our own experiences as educators and what we have learned from them about leadership and the preparation of leaders. Collectively, the four of us have spent nearly two hundred years of residence in and around schools: as students in schools, parents of students in schools, teachers in schools, teachers of teachers, principals of schools, teachers of aspiring and practicing principals for schools, and consultants to schools. We believe these experiences entitle and equip us to dream and design a bit.

The richness of one another's experiences came as no surprise to us. What was surprising was the degree of congruence in what we learned from our very different life experiences. Thus all of what follows is to be prefaced with, "On the basis of our experience, we believe . . ."

Before discussing the preparation of aspiring principals, we first addressed the question, What would we *like* schools of the future to be like? Our first answer was "small." The most powerful learning experiences we observe occur in intimate learning environments of manageable scale. It is virtually impossible to create an effective learning community in a large school. A learning community of three thousand is oxymoronic. To develop effective leaders and effective schools requires personalized scale. It makes little sense to provide distinguished preparation for principals and then place them in huge, institutional settings that nullify their abilities. For us, "small" means from ten to four hundred students and from one to thirty staff members. In such an environment, we believe it possible that intimate, personal, democratic, student-centered learning can flourish.

We also believe that schools of the future must rely more on experiential learning than on didactic teaching. We envision schools as just, moral communities where everyone will be a learner and everyone will be a teacher. We believe that these kinds of schools will be created if, and only if, they have good leaders.

Design Principles

The exciting—and formidable—question the four of us confronted was, How do you select and prepare good leaders for these schools of the new millennium? From our very different life experiences and from our conversations, we teased out a number of pivotal "design principles." These principles now direct our work and characterize the APP.

The Residency

Apprenticeship is a concept that for several centuries has been recognized as the best means for those who don't know how and want to learn how to acquire the characteristics of the accomplished practitioner. Apprenticeship has been around far longer than has formal academic course work. It's time our profession took it seriously.

The residency model has long been recognized by the medical community as an essential means for aspiring physicians to acquire the qualities of an accomplished practitioner. Just as the practicing doctor serves as professor and mentor to the resident who is taking the final steps in becoming a physician, so too can a distinguished principal work closely and continually with an able, bright, motivated educator for a sustained period. In the case of the APP, that period is two years.

The Distinguished Principal

There are approximately one hundred thousand public school principals in the country. A considerable number are truly outstanding educators capable of inspiring others to be equally outstanding. They have become school-based reformers and have built their communities of learners. They have much to teach. The literature on adult development suggests that as all of us approach the zenith years of our careers, we experience a need to pass on what we've done and learned by giving back to others who will succeed us. Experienced, accomplished principals are no different. Under ordinary circumstances, too few principals are able to share their legacy. The distinguished principals are the very heart of the APP. In a real sense, they *are* the APP. By enlisting these educators as mentors for aspiring principals (APs), the program enables the veterans to pass on the wisdom of their craft.

Of equal importance, the APP provides for these seasoned professionals a very sophisticated forum for their *own* professional development. Through writing, conversation, mentoring, and networking, they reflect on and make visible the best of their practice and continually share it with the APs and other distinguished principals. It's difficult for the usual workshop, college course, or in-service to offer significant new learning to the best and the brightest. These individuals have been there and done that. Teaming with other outstanding principals and teaching APs what they know keeps the learning curves of the distinguished principals off the chart and sustains their lifelong learning.

We educators need heroes and role models who are themselves public school educators. Why turn to Welsh of General Electric, Iacocca of Chrysler, or Powell of the military when our profession is populated with genuine folk heroines and heroes? By recognizing these distinguished principals, the program recognizes the profession and draws attention to the wealth of the outstanding figures within it.

The Selection

Only when an AP works in the crucible of the schoolhouse and takes on, little by little, the work of the accomplished mentor—under the continual guidance of the mentor, in constant association with the mentor, and with the enthusiastic support and commitment of the mentor—can we begin in any real sense to "prepare" a principal.

The distinguished principal also *selects*—even recruits—the AP. Who knows better than an experienced principal which members of the faculty are most likely to become outstanding school leaders? These principals have worked closely in the trenches with members of their faculty, through the thick and thin of meetings, parent encounters, classrooms, and playgrounds. Having succeeded in building a learning community, these principals know what it takes to do so. And they know who in their midst has these qualities.

As we saw in the preceding chapter, some teachers have neither the wish to become a principal nor any intention of doing so. Others are already in principal certification programs but may never become outstanding school leaders. Therefore we invite the distinguished principals to identify, from their staffs, one or two teachers who they believe might themselves become distinguished principals. Sometimes this means encouraging those who are not interested; sometimes it means discouraging those who are interested. And sometimes it means influencing the career choice of a teacher. More often it means affirming a teacher's latent, tentative ambition.

Thus, in one way or another, the selection of APs into the program, like much of the content of the program, rests with the distinguished principals. From then on, principal and teacher work closely together in a new way, not as superordinate to subordinate, but as mentor to protégé and as partners in a new learning adventure. In this way, each school grows its own champions.

Common Expectations

We believe that any experience deemed valuable and essential for students is valuable and essential for aspiring and practicing principals. A great leader, like a great teacher, is a great model. Thus, portfolios, exhibitions, writing, teamwork, shared leadership, and community service are experiences as essential for the adults in school as for their students.

The APs, like students in many schools, give presentations of their writings, journals, and projects, which document and demonstrate their work. These exhibitions ensure that the APs are able to reflect on and articulate their work and receive feedback from their mentors, distinguished principals, and other members of the school and APP community. Leaders must walk the talk.

The Schoolhouse

Schools and the communities that surround them can be powerful contexts for student and teacher development. The schoolhouse is also the most promising locus for the development of principals. APs learn how to lead schools by leading schools. They engage in authentic projects, such as building and managing a budget, planning a school or community event, and facilitating staff meetings. This experiential learning offers real-life deadlines and real-life consequences for real-life people.

One AP reflecting on the experience put it this way:

> The Aspiring Principals' Program is real-world training. Each day I have dealt with real situations, from budgeting to community relations, curriculum and assessment issues to staffing and absent teacher coverage. I have worked to bring a diverse group of teachers together around a shared vision. I have challenged the local board of education and district-level administrators on staffing and budgeting issues. These are not textbook or case study scenarios. The people and the problems are real, and I am a direct participant with a vested interest in the outcomes. No other program could offer learning in such a setting.

The evaluation of APs, too, is embedded in the schoolhouse. Each AP is continually critiqued by the teaching staff, by the community, and by the distinguished principal. Because the APs are doing consequential, real work for the school, their assessors are personally invested in holding them to demanding standards.

Integrated Learning

Learning come to aspiring principals in many ways. APs develop leadership skills through continual practice, reflection on practice, and conversation about practice. In addition, there is an important place for booklernin'. It is critical that principals be able to access and make judicious use of the body of educational research.

APs become fluent in the current thinking and writing in their field by identifying a problem—say, the use of standardized tests in promotion of students—and then ferreting out the relevant research literature. In addition, they pursue the problem by visiting other schools and drawing on the abundant craft knowledge within the APP. Every bit as significant to the clarification of an important school issue is their own practitioner-generated research, which they conduct around the problems that concern them.

The kinds of skills and insights needed by the school leader are seldom developed by working in school all day with children and then attending a class on child development at night. All these different knowledge bases about teaching, learning, leadership, and school improvement must be integrated in time and place. The schoolhouse is the place.

Reflecting on Experience

For someone to derive insight and wisdom from experience and subsequently modify practice based on new learning demands intentionality. All school practitioners have experiences—lots of them. Too few experiences are instructive and instrumental in helping improve practice and the practitioner. Promoting adult learning through the experiences acquired in the schoolhouse requires deliberate, rigorous, and imaginative organization and planning.

Because the four of us believe that we learn from experience only if we reflect on our experience, APs engage in many forms of systematic reflection. Writing is a major one. Participants' writing includes a personal journal, submissions to the newsletter that networks the APP, exhibition papers, contributions to published works, and continual correspondence with the partner distinguished principal. For those enrolled in doctoral study, the culminating writing project is the doctoral dissertation, based on the action research conducted during the two years of the program.

For the AP, then, writing is a means of sharing craft knowledge. Writing is an essential leadership skill. And writing offers a record of the participant's work for public dissemination. Above all, writing assists the AP in panning the nuggets from the gravel of experience. Writing brings intention to the experience.

Diversity

As we have seen, in schools educators tend to group out differences as best they can, as fast as those differences appear—differences of ability, social class, special needs, gender—in the name of promoting teacher performance and pupil achievement. My experience in schools suggests that it is *maximizing* rather than minimizing differences among a group of learners that is associated with the steepest learning curves. Embracing differences supports reflection, learning, and the creation of craft knowledge.

A major way that the APP maximizes differences is through the selection of APs and distinguished principals. The first cohort of participants was composed of male, female, black, white, Hispanic, young, and old, all at different stages of their careers. They worked in urban and suburban schools in many states throughout the country. And each participant of course brought to the APP remarkable differences of experience.

Ownership of Learning

One can attempt to teach a student or an aspiring principal, but one cannot learn *for* him or her. We believe that each principal in preparation is ultimately responsible for posing questions and then for designing, fostering, and assessing his or her own learning. It is the responsibility of the APP to support this learning through a network of APs, mentors, assessments, conversations, collective summer experiences, and careful advising. It is important to take inventory continually and to value what each AP already knows and can do, and to assist these educational leaders as they move toward what they do not know and want to know. That is, it is important to treat them like the grown-ups they are.

The Personal Learning Plan

There is another way the program maximizes personal differences. Each AP creates a personal learning plan that includes an assessment of the aspiring leader's skills and gaps in skills as well as the projects and responsibilities he or she intends to take on within the school. The individual learning plan is a way to personalize the program, honor differences, and address the specific learning needs of each AP in relation to the idiosyncrasies of his or her individual school.

As part of her final "exhibition" prior to graduation, one AP presented to others in the program a summary describing her second year's activity based on her learning plan.

List of Amy's Projects and Responsibilities as Aspiring Principal During School Year Sept. 1999–June 2000

Facilitated:

1. Facilitated staff meetings for the entire month of November.
2. Facilitated whole-staff discussion and strategy session on how to combat student drug use.
3. Cofacilitated whole-day meeting on school priorities for next year. Facilitated meetings with parents, students, and advisers when a problem arose and helped create an action plan for how to resolve it.

Created and/or Coordinated for the First Time:

1. Community resource guide based on sixteen interviews with nonprofits and social service agencies in the West End neighborhood.
2. Month-long series of activities and discussions on what it means to be a "peaceful" school.
3. West End Community Clean-up Day when all students picked up trash on ten neighboring streets.

4. International Night—students performed dances and parents cooked food from around the world.

5. Book group for staff on inspiring educational reading.

6. Focus group to study the cases of the students who have left the MET since the school started. The group tried to see what patterns emerged.

7. Student-led PMUs.[2] I train the students to lead the morning meetings every Monday and Friday.

8. Whole-school coverage plan for when an adviser gets sick. I wrote the plan and disseminated it.

9. Training workshop for advisers on drug use among teens.

Ongoing Planning and Leading:

1. Organized and led Buddy Program for parents of new MET students.

2. Taught advisers how to use LTI [Learning Through Internship] project curriculum through role plays.

3. Coordinated Summer Search Scholarship program for whole school.

4. Led the eleventh-grade cross-campus planning meetings and prepared an agenda for each meeting.

5. Planned and cocreated curriculum with other eleventh-grade adviser at my campus.

6. Coplanned all the agendas for weekly staff meetings.

7. Addressed whole student body on issues of theft and drug use.

8. Planned ninth-grade adviser orientation with Jill and Charlie.

9. Outlined roles for next year with Charlie. Compiled detailed list of responsibilities for next year divided among Charlie, Jill, Dennis, Elliot, others, and me.

Emergency Situations:

1. Mediated truces between students in several heated confrontations. Students apologized and shook hands after each mediation.

2. Pursued several middle school students [from another school] who broke windows during our school day.

3. Initiated efforts to meet with the principal of their school on several occasions.

4. Facilitated an investigation by police of a thief who entered the school during the school day.

Human Relations Work with Staff and Students:

1. Helped trouble-shoot logistical difficulties with several MET events.

2. Strategized and created an action plan with school psychologist on how to provide better on-site help to our students.

3. Mentored and coached two first-year advisers.

4. Provided support and guidance to several advisers with their more challenging students.

5. Set up in-school counseling for several students in need.

6. Counseled several students to stay at the MET instead of dropping out to get a GED.

Leader of Events:

1. Led family engagement events, including Family Skills and Talents Fair, Parents of Adolescents Rap Sessions, Family Engagement Committee meetings, and Ninth Grade Parent/Buddy Night.

2. "MC'ed" half of the program for the End of the Year Celebration.

3. Recruited local performers and community role models to speak at morning Pick Me Ups.

Public Speaking:

1. "Education Is Everyone's Business"—cable TV show on family engagement: I spoke about the different family engagement programs that I created at the MET.

2. Harvard University—Debbie Meier and Vito Perrone's class at the Graduate School of Education. I spoke with my student, Cristian Bueno, and researcher, Elliot Levine, about standards for student work at the MET (March 2000).

3. Rhode Island Association for Supervision and Curriculum Development conference—I spoke with my whole advisory in front of one hundred educators about how the MET helps students motivate themselves and set high standards for themselves (April 2000).

4. Harvard University—conference on "Who Will Lead? Crisis in the Principal's Office." I spoke about my experience in the Aspiring Principals' Program.

Weak Learning Plan Areas That I Addressed:

1. School business:

   Attended minority contractors meeting about their role in building the new MET Commons.

Reviewed proposed budget for next year with Dennis and Elliot at an AP meeting and at a MET board meeting.

Observed and participated in meeting with Big Picture business manager about the teacher's pension plan.

Offered input on ongoing facilities discussions regarding the main MET campus.

2. Legal issues:

Reviewed ten cases at AP meeting with Rhode Island Commissioner's chief legal expert.

Communicated with DCYF [Department of Child and Youth Protection Services] for a difficult case of child neglect and truancy. Provided ongoing support and guidance to parent and student.

I doubt that any number of formal courses in a traditional graduate program in educational leadership could have approached Amy's learning, contributions, and satisfaction.

The Present

It is common wisdom that students who constantly see the connection between what they are doing in school and the "real world" are more motivated, learn more, and better retain and value their learning. If students engage in activities that promise to prepare them for some distant, abstract world, their education has little meaning for them. Similarly, if aspiring principals "play school"—read assignments, write papers, take exams—on the assumption that one day this will help them offer outstanding leadership to their schools, they will be disappointed, both as students *and* as school leaders.

For aspiring principals in the APP, school and the real world are synonymous, synchronous, and indistinguishable. Although the purpose is to prepare educators for the principalship, the program isn't only about preparation. The activities are not contrived or incidental. The work must be real and useful, *now*.

The Big Picture

The primary mission of the APP is to select and prepare leaders for schools of the twenty-first century. But in addition to becoming outstanding principals for their schools, leaders also have a responsibility to constantly replenish the profession. Just as teacher leaders contribute to the school beyond their classrooms, so APs contribute to the profession beyond the program. The program provides expectations—and experiences—that link improvement of a public school with improvement of public education. As Amy's exhibition suggests, all distinguished and aspiring principals contribute articles for publication, give talks in public about their participation in the program, welcome visitors to their schools, and are active members of state and national professional organizations.

Midcourse Corrections

A successful program, like a successful leader, must have the ability to constantly observe what is happening, and the adaptability to make changes quickly—in short, to invent on the spot. The best organizations are organic, self-correcting, and self-renewing. Therefore, although the APP has a long-term vision, how to move toward that vision is not carved in stone. Rather, the program proceeds day by day, year by year, taking regular soundings and making changes in response to unexpected problems and opportunities. The dream of tomorrow is more likely to be realized if we do not become so attached to outcomes that we cannot observe, celebrate, and capitalize on what is happening around us today.

We believe that a program that acknowledges, takes seriously, and models these design principles will foster outstanding principals and outstanding school-based reformers, and thereby will foster outstanding schools. Each of the principles I have discussed here is related to creating a culture hospitable to adult as well as student learning, and to the continuation of that learning.

The Experiential Model—Again

As I have suggested, the Transmission of Knowledge model of learning pervades much of formal education. I believe that those who participate in this model—teachers, students, administrators, parents—participate in an activity that appears respectable, rigorous, readily evaluated, and purposeful. The only problem with reliance on the Transmission of Knowledge model is that students (and adults) don't appear to learn very much from it. Or perhaps much is learned that is not intended.

The APP emphasizes less the venerable Transmission of Knowledge model and more the very different Experiential model of learning. Let's look again at the Experiential model, which we first discussed in Chapter Five:

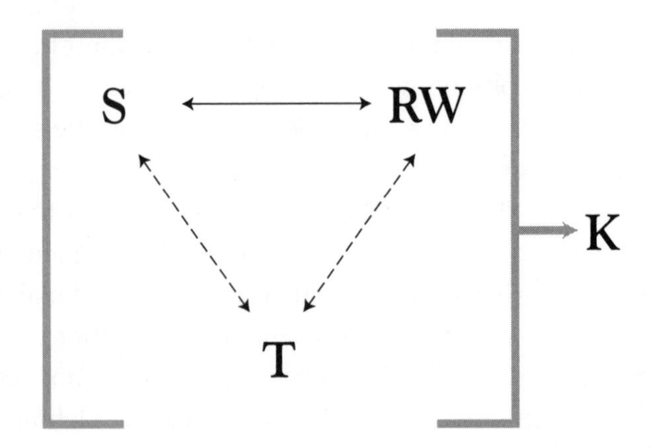

A teacher (T)—or in the case of the APP, usually the mentoring distinguished principal—is instrumental in helping select and provide the pieces of the real world with which the student (in this case, the AP) is occupied or perhaps one day will be occupied. The distinguished principal also offers support, challenge, counseling, a role model, and periodic opportunities to debrief the experience. "How did it go?" "What problems did you encounter?" "What did you learn from the experience?" "How will you do it differently next time?" In short, the "teacher" encourages the "student" to tell stories about the experience and to reflect on, extract, analyze, clarify, and articulate what is being learned from the stories.

Each student (AP) is placed in association with a piece of the "real world." The real world might be a committee of the PTA or a project such as building a school playground. Whereas in most schools the teacher determines the questions for students to pursue, in this model the questions emerge from the interaction of the student with the real world. "Who should be involved in building the school playground?" "Where should it be located?" "Who decides?" "How?" "Is permission needed?" "What is my role?" This is the meaning of ownership of one's own learning, and of experiential learning.

One AP, who had previously been certified in a more traditional program, observed,

> The philosophy of the Aspiring Principals' Program distinguishes itself well above other school leadership programs. We didn't spend our time talking about "what would happen in a school if . . ." or "this is a pretend million-dollar budget, how would you spend your money if . . ." These were the kind of no-risk role-play questions I encountered in courses when I received my first principal certification. It was pencil, paper, and a lot of imagination.
>
> In the Aspiring Principals' Program, we're presented with real-life problems we face in our schools, receive advice and feedback from the participants, and then go back to our schools with action plans. Then we come back to the group and talk about what happened, the future experiences we will have with the people from our schools, and how to continue our work. In my case, I was faced with the responsibility of a true million-dollar budget; my infor-

mation needed to be accurate. No amount of role-playing can truly prepare individuals for the heart-pounding, real-life expectations of being in schools.

From this interaction among student, teacher, and the real world, some knowledge (K) emerges. The nature of this knowledge is not uniform; rather, it is personal and idiosyncratic. From building a playground, one AP may learn new skills in leading a group; from working with a committee of the PTA, another may learn how to differentiate a friendly parent from an unfriendly one.

The Experiential model offers training in independence, not dependence. After living in an experience-rich and learning-filled environment, APs leave "school" able to encounter new situations with confidence and purpose, able to learn from each new encounter with the real world. In short, they become independent, insatiable, lifelong learners.

The Formal Curriculum

The experiences of the AP in the program are anything but random. Behind the program lies a clear set of expectations, a body of knowledge important for every AP to know and to be able to do. In short, there is a curriculum in the more traditional sense. We invited the distinguished principals to reflect on their lifework and tell us what characterizes their exemplary school leadership. These are the elements that they told us constitute best practice and that now form the basis of the curriculum:

Essential Leadership Qualities of Distinguished Principals[3]

- *Human relations and communication.* An exemplary school leader pays attention to the personal. He is thoughtful, understanding, and just. He listens carefully to the thoughts, feelings, and concerns of others. He knows the questions to ask and is able to collect and share information as needed. He is tactful yet direct and has a talent for both one-on-one and group communication. He shows respect for and trust in his staff and promotes the spirit of democratic collaboration. He knows how to support, delegate, and offer input.

- *Moral courage*. An influential principal has the courage to stand alone. She has a commitment, above all else, to doing what is best for children despite the dictates of others. She challenges assumptions and traditions and helps others do so as well.
- *Vision*. An effective school leader must develop and maintain a consistent vision and inspire others to work toward it. He is able to say no to ideas that do not support the vision, for he understands the direction in which the school is moving and is able to predict the desired outcomes.
- *Flexibility and efficiency*. An effective principal is able to juggle many tasks and thoughts at once. She is patient but willing to move, organized, and good at following through on tasks.
- *Lifelong love of learning and leading*. A successful principal creates joy around learning. He deals well with adversity, loves leadership, and thrives on work. He is committed to continual learning and growth for himself.
- *Public support*. A strong principal has a gift for public relations. She is able to present and articulate school results and is an effective fundraiser.

Assessment

Much of this curriculum will inevitably be acquired in the course of the AP's two year's work as intern in the school. Where this is not the case, additional experiences, activities, and readings are devised to ensure competence. It is the responsibility of the distinguished principal, in cooperation with university faculty members, to continually monitor the experiences of the aspirant and to provide additional experiences as needed. And, of course, much will be learned by the APs from their period of residency with the distinguished principal, in addition to this minimum curriculum.

And the learning and accomplishments of the APs can pass muster with state requirements, as another participant notes: "I didn't look at the state competencies before I started my work in the program; but when I completed my internship, I found that I had developed strength in every single competency."

At the end of the two-year program, the distinguished principal and other members of the school community determine if the AP is to be inducted into the principalship. But the ultimate test of the aspirants' success is their performance as leaders in their schools—after they graduate. APs continue to be observed by their mentors after graduating. And, in time, it's expected that many themselves will become distinguished principals in the APP.

The Aspiring Principals' Program[4] does not look or sound much like the school or university with which most of us are so familiar. Having graduated its first cadre of seven certified—and qualified—principals and having received a $1.3 million grant from the Wallace–Readers Digest Funds, the program promises to bring to schools leaders who have experienced powerful, different ways of learning. And these new school principals appear intent on ensuring that youngsters and adults in their schools will experience the same.

School Leadership

Strong school leadership is, and will always be, crucial to educational reform. Yet in this country, the position of school principal is fast becoming a foul-weather job, one few desire and can tolerate. Our nation appears to be moving toward a new definition of school leadership.

The evolving conception, and indeed mandate, for the contemporary principal seems to be the following:

- Do the bidding (and do it well) of superordinates located elsewhere, for example, in the central office, Washington, or Sacramento.
- Comply: agree to take on the goals (and often the means) of those superordinates.
- Believe in their goals (and means).
- Pursue these goals (and means) effectively.
- Agree to be held accountable for attaining their goals, as measured by high-stakes testing.

I find this a frightening, demeaning, and disempowering conception of the role of the school principal, one that has chilling implications for schools. This conception raises for me several questions: Is this leadership? Can any array of carrots and sticks get good, intelligent, people to fulfill this job description? Does anyone want to take on this job description? Even if there are people who do, can anyone really succeed? What kind of schools will result if these principals do succeed . . . or fail? What will children and adults learn in these places?

It's time for a new conception of the school principal, one based on a skilled, passionate, moral commitment to students' and teachers' learning—and to the leader's own learning. Our nation's schools need nothing less than a new cohort of principals who value and trust learning from experience for themselves and who know how to rigorously and courageously craft school experiences such that those experiences yield important personal learning for adults and students alike. Needed now is the courage—and heart—to think and act "otherwise" in order to create in the schoolhouse a culture hospitable to human learning.

12

CONDITIONS FOR LEARNING

> Being the principal learner is the most important thing I can be in my school. —*Dodge Fellow*

Times are changing; schools are changing; school demographics are changing; ideas about what students need to know and be able to do are changing; standards and expectations for schools are changing. Therefore, what school principals do must change as well. Just as the preservice preparation of principals represents one major response to discovering the importance of the principal to schools, so the continuing professional development of practicing principals represents another.

Impediments to Principals' Learning

As we have seen, the most important responsibility of an educator is to model being an active learner, for only when their role models make their learning visible will students take their own learning seriously. This means that every principal must become a lifelong learner. Easier said than done! A host of crippling impediments make it difficult for school principals to become the leading learners in their schools.

Those who try to promote learning for school leaders encounter brick walls as impenetrable as those of the schoolhouse itself. One staff developer once lamented to me, "Give me teachers, parents, even superintendents. But don't give me principals. It's no use. Principals aren't educable." And to be sure, principals who experience attempts to "staff-develop" them as both demeaning and irrelevant resist attempts by others who would inflict their ideas and methods on them. There are good reasons why so many principals are reluctant learners. Some of them are nondiscussables. Most of them are all too common throughout our profession. Principals will become learners only when these barriers are directly acknowledged and addressed.

Time

Many roadblocks stand between a principal and vigorous learning. One of the most common is, "I don't have time. If I attend the workshop after school or if I take part in that summer institute, I'm not going to be able to answer phone calls from concerned parents or prepare the budget for tomorrow's meeting. I don't have time."

When I talk with principals about time constraints, I also hear, "There is no downside for me not spending time on my own learning; nothing bad happens. There *is* a dramatic downside if I don't attend to these hundred other things." As the oxygen mask metaphor suggests, there is of course an *enormous* downside for the educator who neglects his or her own learning. Principals, too, need that oxygen mask.

Old Baggage

A second impediment has to do with the past. Most educators have been the object of somebody's attempt to staff-develop them, whether it's the university, the central office, the state department, or someone else. By and large, this staff development hasn't been very good. "Woefully bleak and miserable" is how one principal described her experience with professional development. Educators don't like to be educated—especially badly. So any fresh invitation to take part as a learner encounters a heavy precedent. We have learned all too well that more of the same is unlikely to help us become better at our work in schools.

Guilt

There is another impediment that stands in the way of educators becoming leading learners in their schools, one that I used to believe was a New England Calvinist affliction but have since found to be more widespread. It is sinful, immoral for an adult to take part as a learner, to snatch bread from the mouths of babes in order to vest himself with precious time and resources. The business of the educator is to serve the learning of others, not to be served. Think of all the paint sets and computers one could buy for the cost of this seminar. Shouldn't we feel guilty?

Still lingering in our profession is a belief that probably emerged from the church of the Middle Ages: that the path to salvation lies in wearing the hair shirt of self-deprivation. "The fact of the matter is," one principal learner observed refreshingly to me, "we just need to take care of ourselves spiritually, physically, and intellectually."

The "Reward" of Learning

To the extent that a principal takes part in a serious learning activity and actually learns something, what is the reward? More work—for both principal and faculty. The reward for the labor of successful professional development for the principal, like the reward for the teacher who becomes a leader, is additional labor. Having learned, the principal must go back to the school and announce to the faculty that she has learned something promising and wants to move in a new and "exciting" direction. "Oh, great!

More work for us." Few will share her excitement. More will display apprehension, resistance, or annoyance. Now she must make midnight phone calls, assure teachers that their place is still safe and that their work in the school is still acceptable and valued.

Principals in their right mind, already overburdened, will think many times before devoting all-too-valuable time to a learning activity the outcome of which, if successful, will demand the expenditure of even more valuable time and effort. The ratio of depletion to replenishment in professional development is one to which we must attend.

Admission of Imperfection

A final impediment to the school principal becoming the principal learner is that by engaging visibly and publicly as a learner, she admits, "I don't know it all." To be a learner is to admit imperfection. Others may even see this as being flawed. "We thought we hired the principal who knew how to evaluate teachers; now you say you must go off to a workshop and learn how? We've made a mistake."

Principals as well as teachers suffer from what one called "a burden of ascribed omniscience." The world thinks you know how to do it all: math, science, PE, social studies, special education. Indeed, many fall into the trap of pretending. School practitioners need to be seen as credible in order to inspire the confidence of students, parents, and teachers. Who inspires more confidence? Who is the better leader? The principal who is learn*ed* and wise or the principal who is a lifelong, insatiable learner?

These are among the impediments that stand in the way of the principal becoming a voracious, public learner. Any one of them is formidable. Taken collectively, they have an especially daunting effect on the capacity of the school principal to be a leading learner. Consequently, in the past, few school leaders have enjoyed a good reputation as learners.

Welcome Developments in the Professional Development of Principals

Happily, the professional development of principals is changing. Stimulated by the renewed recognition of the importance of the principal, the current state of leadership development in this country gives ample cause for not only hope but celebration. Throughout the country, from Iowa to Alaska to Florida to Maine, programs, academies, institutes, principals' centers, and leadership development opportunities have sprung up and are flourishing. Many forge promising new links between the worlds of school, university, government, and business.

Once mired in squabbles about liability insurance and retirement plans, state principals' and administrators' associations, such as those in California and New Jersey, now offer inventive, rigorous, and well-attended summer institutes. State departments of education also are throwing their weight behind the learning of principals. In Missouri, for instance, nine regional principals' academies have been established. Private funders, such as the Danforth, the Carnegie, and the Geraldine R. Dodge foundations, support leadership centers and the learning of school leaders.

Whereas school leaders have formerly been reluctant to commit their insights to the written word, the practice of reflective writing is spreading. The Principals' Institute at Georgia State University, for instance, helps principals write, edit, and publish their work. Colleagues are finding the craft knowledge of fellow school leaders every bit as compelling as the social science research of university people and the pearls of wisdom from business-savvy gurus.

The pedagogy of leadership development has become more adventuresome, more experiential, and less didactic. Activities can include a visit to a poetry festival or participation in Outward Bound and similar adventure programs designed to promote team building, risk-taking, and shared leadership.

And leadership development now extends well beyond national boundaries. Rich activities for school heads can be found, for instance, in the United Kingdom, Canada, Australia, the Netherlands, and Israel. International exchanges among school leaders and workshops are becoming common. The International Network of Principals' Centers at the Harvard Graduate School of Education works to foster such exchanges of ideas and educators.[1]

If the bad news is that principals have less time than ever to devote to their own learning, the good news is that they are *making* time. They no longer need to apologize for including themselves in the learning communities over which they preside. In fact, rather than tiptoeing out the back of the room once they begin a staff development program for others, school principals now commonly participate and model the most important activity of the schoolhouse—learning.

There are all sorts of welcome ripple effects. One principal told me, "Since I joined the Principals' Center, I've noticed that teachers in the building are taking their own professional development far more seriously." It's also clear that when youngsters see learning as something in which important role models engage, they too take learning far more seriously.

This transformation in the role of many school leaders has begun to change schools from places where grown-ups know and young people learn, into communities of learners where all who come under the roof of the school are discovering together the joys, difficulties, and excitement of learning. One principal from New Orleans observed, "As a principal who has fumed under demeaning, mandated staff development, I can say that it feels wonderfully freeing, responsible, and exhilarating to think that we hold in our hands the choice and destiny of our own development."

Herein lies much of the reason for the shift from demeaning to exhilarating leadership development: the ownership of the learning is held in the hands of the principals themselves. When principals pose and address the important issues about which they want and need to know more, they come alive as learners. For when they are responsible for their own learning, principals frequently design activities that they really care about and enjoy, that offer a new angle, that are risky. And they design activities that work.

Learning from the Dodge Fellows

To convey the spirit and the impact of these new efforts in leadership development and to see, in practice, the ideas presented in earlier chapters, I would like here to share an experience from the Principals' Center for the Garden State in New Jersey, an unusual example of what happens when leaders pose and address their own questions and thereby become the head learners in their schools.

In 1992, the Geraldine R. Dodge Foundation initiated a multiyear program intended to promote leadership and learning among the twenty-three hundred public school principals in the state of New Jersey. The foundation invites proposals from principals for a one-year, $5,000 grant. Twenty-five principals are selected each year. Applicants are encouraged to devise and pursue projects that will assist their growth as instructional leaders and thereby, it is hoped, promote the learning of teachers and, ultimately, the learning of students in their schools. An additional grant of $1,000 is awarded to the discretionary fund of the recipient's school. The program has been so successful that it has been repeated every year since 1992.[2]

I serve as a consultant to the project, and every year I spend a day with each cohort debriefing them on their learning experiences. What follows includes the voices of many participating Dodge Fellows during the first five years and my reflections on the program.

For some, it was participation in a summer institute; for others, a cooperative adventure with a colleague; for a few, a trip to explore good schools in foreign lands; yet others immersed themselves in the work of a contemporary figure in education, such as James Comer, Phil Schlechty, or Howard Gardner. Many transformed the Dodge fish and loaf into fishes and loaves by choosing to promote their faculty's professional development along with their own. But all these Fellows had one thing in common: each designed a distinctive "individual educational plan" and pursued it with vigor and inventiveness.

Just as the learning plans principals devised for themselves were idiosyncratic, how much they learned and the nature of that learning varied as well. For most of these educators, the activities in which they engaged clearly constituted remarkable lifetime experiences. One put it this way:

> This was one of the most memorable experiences of my life, not because of what I did, but because of what I learned.[3]

Another commented,

> My husband keeps wondering when I'll be "normal" again.[4]

As participant-observers in this program, the Fellows and I observed powerful, even transformative learning. Some very significant conditions appear to underlie this project, these unusual activities, and this considerable learning. These conditions corroborate much of what we have been discussing in this book, and offer yet another conception of the fertile ground that supports learners and learning.

Recognition

> As middle managers, we are not "first-class citizens," and our work is often bashed or negated.[5]

Few school principals hear an affirmation of their critically important work from the PTA, the teachers' union, or the central office, let alone from the policymakers.

The first word that jumped out at me about the Dodge program was *recognition*, an underlying belief that "we know you principals are out there; we know that you are doing valuable, often heroic work. We value the work you are doing. You are important."

Recognition came in many guises. "You were selected from among twenty-three hundred New Jersey principals" was a big one. The final meeting—not in a linoleum-floored, fluorescent-lit cafeteria but in the elegant home of former presidents of Princeton University—was another. Recognition comes in the different ways that principals were encouraged to write and publish, in the belief that what they have to say—their craft knowledge—is significant and needs to be shouted from the mountaintops. One participant described how she felt this way: "Feeling valued, respected, and worthy of treatment as a first-class citizen."[6] This sense of recognition, I believe, was central in fostering the abundant learning in this program. Perhaps even more important, as another Fellow observed, "this program elevated the significance of the principalship."[7]

Learner-Centered

> The Dodge Fellowship offered me the opportunity to design a customized action plan.[8]

Like the aspiring principals, each of whom devised a personal learning plan, principals in the program selected what it was they wanted to know or to learn more about, based on what they themselves cared passionately about. No one at the Dodge Foundation had a lesson plan mandating that everyone must learn fourteen things. Learning was principal-centered, not prescribed by others. Some selected unusual—even wild—activities that those in universities, state departments, or central offices might have wondered about. Imagine using grant funds to purchase a rototiller to cultivate the school's garden and foster a new curriculum on growing plants! All the participating principals reflected upon themselves as leaders and determined just what it was they wanted to explore in depth and to allocate precious resources to at this stage in their careers. This made a huge difference to their learning.

A Culture of Playfulness

> Big people need to play just as much as little people. It is a child's way of learning. . . . It is the human way of learning.[9]

I found in the activities devised by principals a refreshing culture of playfulness. One brought in a "Dodge ball" to demonstrate support of her learning in the school and the support of her school community. The "class of 1995" referred to themselves as the "artful Dodgers."

There is something in our soul that desperately cries out for playful experiences—for fun. And there is something in most school cultures and within school systems that is toxic to playfulness, particularly in the life of a school administrator. We learned in this experience that a culture of playfulness is closely related to the capacity to learn.

Risk-Taking

> Daring to follow my heart along with my head. . . . I now find it much easier to disregard that negative, internal voice of judgment which either whispers or thunders, "Don't try that. You know it won't work. It's never been done that way before. It's an eccentric idea which bodes only ill."[10]

Another quality evident in the work of principals in the Dodge program was a willingness to take risks—often great risks. Each participant took a risk by publicly identifying himself or herself to a school community as a learner. Doing so is every bit as risky as a bungee jump!

Participants risked by standing before two dozen peers and saying, "Here's who I really am; here's what I learned over the course of a year." The foundation, and the culture of support developed within the group, provided a belaying line that both modeled and enabled risk-taking—for some, risk-taking beyond what they had ever experienced. For many, willingness to risk within the program transferred back to the schoolhouse:

> Dispensing with the regular schedule and creating weeklong interdisciplinary units was risk-taking.[11]

Staff development for educators must be characterized by risk-taking—and safety straps.

Visibility as a Learner

> My teachers see me as a learner, and I am proud of that. When I am out of the building for a day to "learn," I include in my daily journal to the student body: "I am at a meeting today learning about technology. I can't wait to come back and share what I have learned!" The Dodge Foundation and the Principals' Center have enabled me to become a learner again and to model the concept of lifelong learning to the school community.[12]

Related to risk-taking, of course, is visibility as a learner. Most of the participants' school communities learned of their grant, that it was intended to promote their principal's professional development and that their school leader was pursuing a self-constructed learning design.

By declaring oneself a learner, one invites the question, So what have you learned? What are you learning? One must then *be* a learner and disclose this learning to others. Usually, the principal holds students' and teachers' feet to the fire and expects them to be learners. In the Dodge program, the situation was reversed: Students and teachers track their principal's learning. Where did you go? What did you learn? In this way, the leader's learning became a discussable. I suspect that this visibility contributed not only to the principals' learning but also to others' learning.

That You Are Learning, What You Are Learning

> I once thought that school was about teaching "what to think." I now see it as teaching "how to think." I once saw it as "mind stuffing," "word swallowing," and I now see it as something to do with the "pursuit of wisdom" and "mind building." That shift . . . has had a profound effect on the programs that we have undertaken in our school.[13]

For an educator, *that* she is learning is every bit as important as what she is learning. In our schools, we are so preoccupied with "what" youngsters are or are not learning—fractions or the planets or parts of speech—or with what principals are learning—budgeting, teacher evaluation, plant management—that we're oblivious to them being alive (or dead) as learners. Yet, as we all know, a precondition for any of us to learn anything is that we must be ignited by learning. Then and only then can we successfully bring ourselves to a host of new subjects or questions as inquirers.

What each principal learned in this program was, of course, of great value—whether it was about experiential science teaching, about cooperative learning, or about Mortimer Adler. But *that* they were (and still are) learning, I believe, has even more import—and shelf life.

As I have noted, one definition of an at-risk student is any student who leaves school before or after graduation with little possibility of continuing learning. Applying that definition, I fear our schools are all too full of at-risk students and at-risk teachers and administrators. We must give as much attention to ensuring that we are all learning, that we know how to learn, that we are committed to our lifelong learning, as we give to *what* we are all supposed to be learning.

Constructing One's Own Knowledge

A popular phrase in our current educational discourse is *constructing your own knowledge*, reflecting the belief that students learn more when they are creating their own learning opportunities rather than being the passive recipient of another person's expertise. From the stories of the Dodge Fellows, it is apparent that over several months, they assembled brick by brick their own hard-won insights about computers and technology, about gardening, about multiple intelligences, about a hundred fields of inquiry. Rather than merely being taught, rather than placing the burden on another to teach them, they took responsibility for constructing their own knowledge about whatever it was they had set about to learn. Consequently, what each built continues to have special meaning and import.

Incorporating the Liberal Arts

> I was a liberal arts major in undergraduate school and always felt this was a real advantage when I became a teacher, guidance counselor, and principal. I also felt that many of my school colleagues were "disadvantaged," having gone the sterile route of teachers' college, methods courses, and one-shot staff development activities. Through the inspiration provided by Dodge, I tried to shift the focus at school. Our cultural programs include more high-quality literature, music, poetry, storytelling. Our librarian, teachers, and parents work hard to acquire outstanding literary acquisitions for our media center. Discussions in the faculty room frequently center on good books, theatre, concerts, rather than the usual gripe sessions. Teachers frequently propose activities and initiatives that support the liberal arts.[14]

The culture created by the foundation and the Fellows expanded the often technocratic, sterile field of education to include the liberal arts. No longer disjointed (as represented in universities by a school of education and a college of the liberal arts), these two worlds became integrated. Principals talked about and engaged in dance, poetry, literature, history, and philosophy. And, for many, this expanded conception of learning continues:

> I have made time in my demanding schedule to attend more lectures, concerts, theatre, and museum exhibits, and to read more contemporary literature as well as reread classics.[15]

Education joined with the liberal arts (or, even better, never having been severed from them) becomes more exciting and rich.

Inventive Irreverence

Conventional wisdom tells principals to run their schools to maximize order and minimize dissonance—and thereby to minimize the number of problems that land on the superintendent's desk. In many of the learning projects designed by the principals, we saw a quality of constructive irreverence. The Fellows often made choices and pursued learning, unimpeded by convention.

One courageous pair of principals worked together toward a goal of interracial understanding within and between their schools; they found that great learning is often accompanied by great dissonance, and even by many phone calls to the central office. Many principals discovered that challenging authority, pushing limits, breaking the frame, and "being themselves" in inventive, responsible ways (often at considerable risk), contributed to profound learning, if not order and comfort, for everyone. They were thinking otherwise.

A *Sense of Wonder*

> An important part of our work as school principals is to facilitate dreams. The Dodge grant helped us become dreamers.[16]

Schools can become quite arid, unimaginative, and routinized organizations that provide youngsters and grown-ups alike an uninspired and uninspiring diet. Each of us entered the world with a magical, even spiritual sense of wonder—wonder about the universe, about ourselves, about those around us. We were blessed with the poetry of life. Somehow, over the years, that precious sense of wonder is neglected, abused, devalued, or extinguished within the family, the neighborhood, the school, or the workplace. Fortunately, for all of us the embers of wonder continue to burn beneath the surface. Just as a sense of wonder can provoke learning, so too can learning fan these coals and restore our sense of wonder.

We have all heard about "teachable moments." I think many people observed in these Dodge activities that when a sense of wonder is unlocked—about fractals, the painting of Whistler's mother, or zucchini plants—our spirits come alive and we experience a "learnable moment." One participant observed that in the Dodge program, "We had the food for soul, body, and mind."[17]

High Expectations

> We were challenged beyond what we thought we could do.[18]

The literature of the effective schools movement lists "high expectation of students" as one of the five cardinal prerequisites for student achievement, and for good reason. We tend to live up to—or down to—the expectation of those we care about and respect.

Most of the Fellows responded with great success to the program's many challenges, whether these came from the Dodge Foundation, from within themselves, or both. If others believe I can fly, and I suspect I can fly, chances are I can fly. Thus, for these learning principals, the high expectations of others, of the school community, and of fellow principals, and their high expectations of themselves, seem every bit as related to their learning as our high expectations for youngsters are related to theirs. One inventor put it something like this: If you think you can—or if you think you can't—you are right.

Collegiality

> Collegiality is an essential part of growing and developing.[19]

In the school world, relationships tend to be independent and isolated, or adversarial and competitive. So it is for all too many principals. They live in what one called "our separate caves."

Working alone is good for neither the quality of the product nor the quality of life of those who produce the product. In contrast, many wonderful, fresh ideas emerge when two or three educators brainstorm and bounce ideas off one another. As we observed in the Aspiring Principals' Program, a small group will usually generate richer and more unusual ideas than will any one of its members working alone.

Participants in the Dodge program found and created what one called *a culture of collegiality*. One principal observed,

> I never dared speak about my learning back home. Other principals in the program and I can now communicate and speak the same language.[20]

Most came to realize that isolation and competition are inhospitable to learning. Learning is frequently a social activity. Working in schools is depleting. Working alone in schools is even more depleting. Working and learning together in schools can be replenishing.

Reflection

> This experience promotes reflection. Sometimes we're so busy running we forget to stop and think about it. We have not only been thinking about it; we talk to people about what we're thinking.[21]

Many of the participants were struck by the metaphor of a school as a ballroom floor, with the principal enthusiastically dancing in the midst of it all. But they also recognized the crucial need to find moments to ascend to the balcony and observe and reflect on what is happening below on that dance floor. During the many months of the program, principals reflected on their practice—ascended to the balcony—by talking with one another in conversation, by telling stories, by writing, by walking, by allowing themselves to be consumed by a sense of wonder. The reflective practitioner is, above all, a learning practitioner.

Self-Assessment

> It's been like taking a course and not having to take the exam. It's been fun.[22]

Our profession is preoccupied by assessment and evaluation: assessment—by someone else—of students' learning, of teachers' teaching, and of principals' leadership. Rigorous, external assessment is thought to promote learning and be good for humans and other living things. However, many principals in this program experienced delight that they, not the foundation or the superintendent or the board of education, determined how successful this adventure in learning had been.

One of them thanked the foundation

> for giving us reason to dream and the support to make these dreams reality, and not demanding measurable results.[23]

Does the money spent paying off that rototiller, which was an integral part of bringing the growth of plants into the school's curriculum, represent a more or less "legitimate" expenditure than the money spent to fly to Germany to visit a remarkable school or the money invested in a summer institute at Vanderbilt? Only the learner knows. Each participant monitored his own learning and asked himself, Did I get anything out of this? Am I learning? What am I learning? And how can my learning be put to good use in school? Self-normed and relieved of an outside agent placing a judgment on their learning, most of the school principals reported that their learning curves went up rather than down.

Authenticity

> I became aware that I could become myself as a principal. "Be yourself" was not a message I heard when I assumed the principalship. At first I tried to act the way I thought a principal should. Then I tried to become the principal my superintendent thought

> I should be. The commonality of our work in the program, accompanied by the differences in our personalities, provided the strength that I needed to help me say, "This is for me. I can be me and still be a principal without losing my identity."[24]

Another buzzword in our profession is *authentic assessment;* to be sure, authentic assessment is preferable to inauthentic or contrived assessment. Yet I wonder, how authentic is the learning we want to authentically assess? And how authentic are the learners? I believe authentic assessment of contrived learning is only partway there. Still needed are authentic learners who are authentically learning and are authentically assessed, preferably (as we saw in the Aspiring Principals' Program) by themselves, with the support and encouragement of those who would facilitate their learning. One principal observed,

> As a school leader . . . I share more of myself.[25]

It became evident to all of us associated with this project that the "real me" was showing up. Something about these activities allowed principals to participate fully, to reveal themselves, to disclose, and not to check that real me at the door, as the job so often demands we do (or as we suppose that it does).

When the learners were authentic, the learning became authentic because it was self-constructed, related to practice, accompanied by a sense of wonder, and not confined to the field of education. I suspect that the unusual level of learning also had much to do with the integration of personal and professional development.

Intersection of the Personal and the Professional

> Being a Dodge recipient has been a personal and a professional growth experience for me.[26]

Most funds or activities dedicated to promoting principals' learning are targeted for *professional* development—building new skills at budgeting, evaluating teachers, developing curriculum, introducing portfolios. Implicitly (and sometimes explicitly) ruled out is support, encouragement, or even the acknowledgment of principals' *personal* development, in which category we might include the capacities to express feelings, to be vulnerable, to demonstrate confidence, to take risks, to trust.

As learners, we are not bifurcated into two neat hemispheres, one called professional, one called personal. To the contrary, learning is holistic. Each of us comes in one package. I believe that until we acknowledge and honor a large element of personal growth in our learning activities, there won't be much professional growth. This is precisely why so many professional development activities are so forgettable. How different was the experience of one participant:

> I believe that my own learning has "gone off the chart" because of the personal nature of the experiences . . . offered us. . . . You treat each of us as a unique individual. You always have a positive and personal comment for each of us.[27]

Many discovered that profound learning is a wondrous experience that occurs at the intersection of the personal and the professional.

Variety

> There has been such an amazing diversity of opportunities and experiences.[28]

Despite ability groups, interest groups, the "shopping mall high school," and attempts at individualized instruction, our school world reveals racks and racks of shoes thought to fit all—an 8:30 to 3:00 day; report cards; taking five subjects; and for fifty-five minutes taking notes, writing reports, reading books, and taking exams. All students (and grown-ups) in school are required to live and learn within a homogenized environment.

The experience of the principals involved in the program dramatically confirms the value of *differences* as a condition associated with profound learning. We experienced diversity among the different learning proposals, diversity in the activities principals chose to pursue and in the form of pedagogy each principal found most useful. Reports were full of accounts of reading, writing, traveling, working alone, working with others, constructing one's own activities, and attending activities designed by others. Some of the activities in which principals engaged were low in risk, others were high in risk. Clearly, principals have preferred learning styles, which when matched with compatible learning environments can lead to unusual levels of learning.

And there was variety among the participants; these women and men came from rural, urban, and suburban schools, from elementary, middle, and high schools. There were beginning principals and experienced principals; there were African American, white, and Hispanic principals. Many reported the value of participation with very different others who do the same work but in very different kinds of workplaces.

> Expanding my personal circle of peers to include people in quite different settings provides a forum for lively discussion, professional partnerships, and personal reflection.[29]

The Dodge experience suggests that it is maximizing rather than minimizing differences among a group of learners that seems to be associated with the steepest learning curves.

• • •

These are the conditions that, as one principal observed, "facilitated an awakening of education among principals across the state."[30] Certainly, individual principals found some of the conditions to be more salient than others, and there were also undoubtedly other factors at work; but there is ample evidence that these conditions characterized the learning environment created by and for this group of educators. It is important to note that these conditions seldom occurred discretely, in isolation from one another. As one participant observed, "I found [these conditions] strongly interactive, interdependent, and intertwined."[31]

What is the significance for principals of enumerating these seventeen conditions? First, drawing attention to them may help these and other school leaders provide these conditions for themselves—help them don that oxygen mask. If principals are committed to becoming lifelong learners, they must assume responsibility for identifying and providing the conditions that nourish their learning. The central office or the university is not going to do that for them. Whether we find that all, some, or few of these conditions are associated with learning, it is important to realize that there *are* conditions that ignite each principal as a learner and thereby transcend the many impediments to learning.

There is a second reason to highlight these conditions. This Dodge Foundation program was intended to promote the development of school principals as instructional leaders, on the assumption that their learning might, in turn, affect others throughout each school community. Even though neither the Dodge Foundation nor the participating principals formally undertook to show that good things were happening to others in the schools as a result of principals' learning, it is important to acknowledge what conversations and the writing of these principals reveal: that when adults visibly behave and learn in the ways suggested in this chapter, ripple effects do seem to radiate throughout the schoolhouse for teachers, students, and perhaps parents. One principal told this story:

> I started to write just for my own personal benefit. I distributed most of my writing to our staff and parents. This has produced a wonderful side effect. My teachers know that I write, and now some of them do too. Our whole school family knows what I think about a variety of issues.[32]

A kind of modeling effect seems to have been operating:

> I internalized that creative model and in turn modeled it for . . . the staff, who modeled it for our students. What a transformation![33]

> Learning is contagious, and it has spread to my staff. . . . I felt it important to provide the same professional feeling I have received from Dodge.[34]

There is a third reason to note the seventeen conditions. The learnings that have emerged from the Dodge experience may have wider import. I believe we have begun to uncover, affirm, and refine some of the most important conditions under which not only these one hundred principals but also other human beings learn best and most.

Let's look again at the conditions. Many would say, "Well, yes, of course. These are the conditions hospitable to human learning. Of course." But why, then, are they so dramatically unrecognized and conspicuously absent in so much of the thinking and practice in state departments of education, central offices, universities, and all too many schools—all institutions professing a commitment to promoting human learning?

If the work of a school-based reformer is to create a culture hospitable to human learning, then every educator must ask the following questions:

1. Am I conveying to students and teachers and parents a sense of recognition, a feeling of their importance?
2. To what extent am I identifying and selecting what it is I care passionately about learning? Am I enabling others to do the same?
3. Would I characterize my school as one that offers a culture of playfulness?
4. Do I value and place a premium on risk-taking by others? Do I provide a safety strap to those who risk?
5. Who are those who model voracious, passionate learning in my schoolhouse? To what extent am I such a role model?
6. Am I placing as much emphasis on the fact that students and teachers are learning as on what they are supposed to learn?

7. To what extent am I creating the conditions that allow others to construct their own knowledge? To what extent am I attempting to impart—even inflict—my knowledge on them?
8. Is the education I provide for young people and grown-ups in my school inclusive of all the domains of learning, or have I selected only some portions and excluded others?
9. Would I describe my school or classroom culture as one that supports inventive irreverence?
10. Would I describe my school or classroom culture as one that fosters a sense of wonder?
11. Do I have high expectations that all students and all teachers and all parents—and I, myself—can be profound learners, or do I think of some as learners and others as in the "bottom ability group"?
12. Are the relationships among the students and among the adults in my school collegial? Or are they isolated, competitive, adversarial?
13. Do I and my school provide for the younger and older learners assembled there a climate conducive to reflection? Are there opportunities to reflect?
14. Do I give respect and attention to the internal assessment by learners themselves as well as to external assessments?
15. To what extent is my school culture one that promotes authenticity? Are the "real me's" showing up among the teachers and students, or are they being checked at the door each morning?
16. To what extent do I honor the personal development as well as the professional development of students and teachers? Are these seen as separate or integrated objectives?
17. In my school, do I attempt to maximize the variety of activities, formats, pedagogies, learning environments, and people? How wide and inclusive is that variety?

There are many ways principals and other school people can respond to these questions, as a high school teacher, a department chair, and a principal in Portland, Oregon, suggest.[35] They have written, for example, that "An authentic way to show staff members that their work and ideas are valued would be to ask for a wish list from each department chair or team leader at the beginning of the school year and to use it in planning and budgeting." A way to emphasize *that* teachers and students are learning as well as *what* they are supposed to be learning would be for "leaders . . . [to] ask teachers to base one of their yearly professional goals on their own learning interest. . . . This could give teachers and principals another opportunity to converse about what they are learning from each other." Conditions can be created that allow others to construct their own knowledge "by facilitating work sessions in which teachers synthesize theory and make specific applications for their own schools, disciplines, grade levels, and classrooms."

A story is told at Princeton, the home of Albert Einstein. Someone once asked the great scientist what it was like to know all there is to know about math and science. Einstein reportedly answered, "I don't know all there is to know. In fact, I have been learning all of my life—except for the interval I spent in school." If in our schools we can create the conditions that the Dodge Fellows helped to uncover, then students and their educators will find profound learning in those intervals spent in school.

13

SOME QUESTIONS

> This is the true joy in life, the being used for a purpose recognized by yourself as a mighty one; the being a force of nature instead of a feverish selfish little clod of ailments and grievances complaining that the world will not devote itself to making you happy. —*George Bernard Shaw*

In its own way, each of the foregoing "case studies" offers a partial promise of reforming American education. The work of the Rhode Island Foundation with teacher leaders, the Aspiring Principals' Program, and the leadership development program of the Dodge Foundation and Principals' Center for the Garden State all exemplify concepts essential to building a community of learners and a community of leaders.

And each puts into practice many of the principles of school-based reform that we considered at the outset. We see in these three efforts teachers and principals becoming leading learners—even life-long learners—because of their commitment to abundant observation, reflection, writing, conversation, and storytelling and because of their respect for differences and craft knowledge. By employing the Experiential model of learning, each program challenges participants to "think otherwise." As a result, they experience transformative as well as informative learning, which will assist them in

becoming school-based reformers. In short, these three programs manifest the very qualities I dream that one day every school and every school system will come to display: community, learning, and leading.

Thus far, this book has been composed largely of conversations I have had with school educators. In this chapter, I would like to have a conversation with you, the reader. I assume that if you have gotten this far, you are prepared to advance even further into the arena of school reform. To that end, allow me to ask several critical questions that will, I hope, provoke and support you and clarify your important work.

By school reform I mean fundamental, systemic, and sustained change that will transform schools into communities hospitable to human learning. The practitioners I know who have experienced the most success in moving toward school reform focus on these questions, wrestle with them, and then deal with them. They are tough questions for you who would reform your schools. Very tough. Let me try to frame them so that you too can focus on them, wrestle with them, and perhaps deal with them.

Question 1: Who Are the School-Based Reformers?

This volume is largely about and addressed to teachers, principals, and other school professionals like you. Yet this is not to suggest that you are the only ones who reside under the roof of the schoolhouse or that you are the only ones capable of seeing the need for, initiating, and carrying out school reform. For instance, in many schools parents now sit on school site councils, hire and fire principals, evaluate teachers, and develop curriculum. They are at least as heavily invested in the success of the school as you are because they are heavily invested in the success of their own children. I know. For fourteen years I was a card-carrying member of the PTA. I was part of that cadre that our exasperated principal once called "severely gifted parents."

As principal, I daily witnessed parents contributing to the improvement of the school in significant ways: staffing the library, driving on field trips, making costumes for school plays, serving on curriculum committees—indeed, serving on the committee that appointed me.

One parent, Ellie, I remember with especial reverence. She took on what seemed like the thankless job of starting and then managing a weekly school newspaper, read by students, their parents, faculty, and educators in other schools. For many years, spanning her own children's school careers, she used this position to get people to talk together who normally didn't. She made visible many of the impressive things going on in classrooms—and some of the unimpressive things. She raised questions about the school that needed to be raised—and addressed. She challenged the principal's encrusted policies. Through her precision in editing and writing, she modeled a level of literacy to which the rest of us could only aspire. The power of the press! Can parents be school-based reformers? You bet.

Much has rightly been made of the importance of parent involvement to the success of school improvement. Little, however, has been written about the importance to school reform of the major clients of the schooling enterprise—the students. Nothing prevents students from being seen as or from becoming school-based reformers—except past and present practice.

It's surprising that more attention has not been accorded to students as change agents within schools. Students would seem likely partners in this enterprise for several reasons: there are *many* of them. In every school I know, students outnumber adults at least ten to one. And students have apparently endless energy. Stand at the schoolhouse door at dismissal time. Students explode out of the building with the same energy with which they arrived—if not more.

An hour or two later, teachers and administrators drag themselves out of their classrooms and offices, stumble into the parking lot, and slouch into their cars. If they had to walk home, few would make it. And yet it is on top of the existing responsibilities of teachers and administrators, whose plates are full, that the responsibility for school reform is placed. Something's wrong with this picture.

And of course students are vitally invested in improving their schoolhouse because, unlike so many others who would reform the school, they *live* in that house.

In our profession we often say that all decisions are, or should be, made in the best interests of pupils. If large numbers of students, possessing enormous kinetic energy and unique insights about the effects of the school experience upon them, could be enlisted as architects, engineers, and designers of schools—watch out.

I remember the snowballs. Every time it snowed in Boston, we had a problem. I dreaded the annual arrival of the white stuff. Kids on the playground would throw snowballs. Invariably a window or a nose would be broken. Then there would be an upset child, a call home, and a visit from an upset parent. Or an upset teacher. Then there was an upset principal.

What usually happens in these and similar situations in schools is that everyone looks to the principal for a solution. The principal then attempts to post adult guards around the playground to ensure adequate protection and coverage. In most schools, no teacher in her right mind would agree to such a job description during precious recess time. Therefore, what happens next is a meeting and then the creation and imposition of a rule intended to rectify the situation and protect teachers' time: "No snowballs" and "No going outside when it's snowing or when there is snow on the ground."

As an inveterate snowballer, I found these and similar "solutions" anti-life. When one fourth grader moaned, "When it snows, you *have* to throw snowballs," I had to agree. So I got together after school with some youngsters who, like me, believed in the natural right of snowballers and in the inherent worth of throwing snowballs. I told them that if they could devise a plan that permitted snowballs and solved the problems of people getting hurt, of angry parents, and of additional teacher supervision, we would go with it. These formidable conditions did nothing but pique their interest and stimulate their brainstorming. Much more fun than a computer game, this was for real!

Two days later, four boys and two girls appeared in my office with a wonderful, inventive plan: they would set up a "combat zone" in the field, marked by four corner pylons connected by trampled lines in the snow. Anybody who went inside the combat zone could throw snowballs and be hit by snowballs—with abandon. Anybody who didn't want to throw or be hit stayed outside the boundaries, where "No snowballs" was the rule. If you were hurt in the zone, you were not allowed to call home or come crying to the principal's office. By going into the zone you took full responsibility for whatever happened. (I sought no legal counsel on the question of signing away liability!)

The new policy was duly announced in assembly and printed in Ellie's school newspaper for all to see. It caused lots of talk and interest in the faculty room . . . and around dinner tables in town. But no complaints, only intrigue.

A week later, the heavens exploded with six inches of new snow—an opportunity to inaugurate the new plan. The kids went into action, setting up the posts and tramping the boundaries. Several tough youngsters immediately entered the combat zone and started pummeling one another. The timid stood at the boundary and watched. Many more boys and girls jumped in and then immediately jumped out. The new sport worked beautifully, for the bold and the timid alike.

The students were happy, the teachers were happy, the parents were happy, and the principal (who also spent some time in the combat zone) was happy. Students, too, can think otherwise!

Were those six youngsters school-based reformers? Reflecting, having conversations, dreaming a better way, working together, providing leadership to implement that better way, monitoring it? Transforming the school's culture into one of risk-taking, playfulness, and respect for differences? You bet.

But alas, student councils notwithstanding, student perspectives are largely absent in the important deliberations about school problems and the invention of better ways. Such consequential issues as school or classroom rules, teacher evaluation, design of curriculum, pedagogy—and school improvement—are off-limits to most of the clients of most schools. By depriving youngsters of participation, we deprive ourselves and the school of their inventive ideas. We deprive youngsters of vital preparation for the real world, where they will be expected to participate and contribute.

It need not be so. In a few schools, I've seen elementary and middle school pupils, as well as high school students, contribute to school reform efforts in a variety of ways:

- Students give feedback to the educators and sometimes engage in more elaborate forms of practitioner research. They are asked, What teaching styles work for you? How do you experience the culture of this school? What times of day do you learn best? By giving such feedback, students help generate new knowledge as well as become the beneficiaries of the findings of others.
- Students participate in decision-making bodies charged with monitoring and improving the health of the school. They work alongside educators to make decisions about hiring a new teacher, devising a pupil evaluation system, holding parent conferences, or planning a night for their parents.
- Students provide expertise and implement change. Many students, for instance, are at least as capable with computers and technology as those charged with teaching them about computers and technology. A team of students can mastermind a new block schedule or the design for a new computer lab as well as can most educators. They have much to bring to a collaborative effort.

I find that we adults are reluctant to let students sit at the table with us in these and other ways because we feel that their attendance will be unreliable, that they will bring nothing to the conversations unknown to adults, or worse, they may bring better ideas than the adults' and make us feel inadequate. Furthermore, they will act in irresponsible ways (that is, attempt to undermine or overthrow the control of the adults).

Just as the students who were invited to take responsibility for a snowball policy welcomed and made prudent use of the opportunity, so it is when we invite students to show responsibility for the larger learning environment of the school. Sharing leadership need not stop with teachers.

When I talk with educators who have enlisted students as first-class citizens of, say, a school site council, most report that students' attendance is at least as reliable as that of the grown-ups (often more!), that many students have novel and valuable insights to offer, and that most act very responsibly. It appears that students live up to our high expectations of them—or live down to our low expectations.

If serious school-based reform is to occur, we educators cannot afford to neglect any human or material resource. We will have to be inventive and courageous in enlisting all the help and energy we can muster from all quarters. We must do so even when we are unsure of the outcome—of just where those snowballs will go. Students, like their parents, offer an astonishing potential for school improvement—free.

So, who gets to play? Who will be included in *your* school as school-based reformers?

Question 2: What Is the Logic Behind Reforming Your School?

A vision is a conception of a desired future. A logic represents the assumptions and organizing principles for getting there. If what, then what? "If we do ABC, then we expect DEF will happen." What are the ABCs and the DEFs? A clear logic is not apparent to me in most school reform efforts. Possibly because there is no clear vision, there is often not one logic but several, all tangled and confounded. Let me try to disentangle a few I have observed.

- *Kick-the-radio logic*. Schools, especially urban schools, are seen as so helpless, so hopeless, so broken that there's little to lose by giving them a good, hard kick. To use a dated metaphor, it's like kicking a broken radio. Perhaps the tube filaments will align by chance in a different way, and the radio will work. In any case, since it's already broken, what is there to lose? I see elements of this logic in some legislation born of frustration. The Chicago School Reform Act of 1988, for instance, was seen by many as kicking the radio.
- *Sled-in-the-ice logic*. Some see schools as similar to sleds frozen in ice. They hope that small pushes and tugs—forty-five-instead of fifty-five-minute periods, 200 days a year instead of 186, new math texts instead of old—will one day move the sled forward. But this is mere tinkering. Many believe that the schools cannot reform. Incremental change is for schools that need refinement; massive intervention is for schools that need reform. A critical jolt is needed to dislodge the sled.
- *Everybody-wins logic*. Schools are highly political institutions, full of groups interested in their own agendas. The reason schools are so mired in what Theodore Sizer calls sustained paralysis is that there is a fear that any change will adversely affect *some* group, which will, in turn, thwart the change. Is it possible for fundamental change to be linked with desirable outcomes for *everyone*—recognition, compensation, dignity, participation? A head teacher's position with a salary of $70,000 a year, lead teachers, parent involvement, shared decision making, student government? The logic: if there is something in it for everyone, then no one will sabotage promising new ideas, and schools will change.
- *Business logic*. American businesses are outpacing the rest of the world. Therefore, the way to reform a school is to run it more like a business: with teamwork, quality control, competition, productivity, measurable results, focus on the bottom line, and highly disciplined workers.

Although they are seldom explicit, these are all logics I have observed operating in efforts to improve schools, and I'm sure there are more logics or logic fragments out there. But I believe that the most important logic behind the success of a school's reform effort is the logic of that school's own members. There is a pressing need to spell out our assumptions about schools as organizations, about people, about learning, about the purpose of education, about the future. Each school needs to formulate a logic unique to its reform effort. In order not to be muddled in the plethora of logics out there, every school needs its own. I'm convinced that a school can develop and clarify its logic about change, articulate it, and continually scrutinize and refine it.

So, what is *your* school's logic about change, on which you will rest efforts at reform?

Question 3: Do You Really Believe Your School Needs a Complete Overhaul?

Many educators lay much of the responsibility for the ills of our schools on the ills of society. But I sometimes wonder if we have a poorly functioning society because we have a dysfunctional school system. To what extent are you contemplating reform because *you really believe* that the way you go about teaching or running a school needs a complete overhaul? To what extent are you restructuring because external forces—businesses, legislatures, and national commissions—tell you to do so? The structure of schools hasn't changed much in 150 years. If we educators really believed schools needed an overhaul, why haven't we done anything before? If there were no external heat, would the reform pot be boiling today?

I once read somewhere that about 75 percent of the teachers and administrators polled thought schools in the United States were in deep trouble and in need of fundamental change. But fewer than 25 percent of the same sample felt that their own school was in any serious difficulty. These numbers don't add up. Perhaps reform is like a nuclear power plant—a good idea, but not in my backyard? Or could it be, as one mother and teacher observed, that the only person who welcomes change is a wet baby?

The nation's schools that have gone furthest toward reform are in urban districts, such as Chicago, Miami, Milwaukee, and Rochester. What about those in suburban or rural areas where many people think schools are performing adequately? What about independent schools? Do you really believe *your* school needs a rebuilt engine and chassis—or just an oil change? The implications of believing that only other schools are in trouble or that reform is necessary only at gunpoint have obvious consequences for the future of reform. Is your school "broken"? Do you believe that it needs to be fixed? This leads me to a fourth question.

Question 4: Teachers and Administrators, Are You Prepared to Acknowledge Your Contributions to the Problems of Schools and to Change Your Assumptions and Practices?

Poorly performing, at-risk students, teachers, and administrators don't exist in a vacuum. Every schoolhouse teems with interactions, conversations, and events. A schoolhouse is a dynamic environment, and you are a major participant. What you *choose* to do, randomly or thoughtfully, has the potential to profoundly affect the lives of the children and adults around you.

Look in the mirror. Reflection begins with the self. Are you prepared to reflect on how you have become part of the problem of the school you want to reform? And are you prepared to reflect on how you will become part of the solution?

On a trip to Alaska I was deeply moved to hear an Inuit elder from a small tribe lament,

> Before our people went to school, we worked together hunting a seal or skinning a caribou. In school we learned that to cooperate is to cheat. Before the schools came we were a spiritual people.

> We had reverence for life. Indeed, the essence of our life was spiritual. Now everything is cognitive. Our children used to dance and celebrate and be filled with joy. Now they must sit still in their seats where they face a never-ending parade of abstract learning and symbols.

After hearing these words, I reflected on those things I had done in my life as a teacher and administrator that I ought not to have done and on those things I had not done that I ought to have done.

This story offers a metaphor that schooling may be, in many ways, a *subtractive* process that forces students to give up their cultures, relinquish their creativity, and demean themselves in order to succeed or to merely survive.

One major purpose of schooling is thought to be to take youngsters at risk and, through a variety of interventions, remove them from this peril—and to prevent others from ever becoming at risk. Many have attempted to figure out exactly what causes students at school to become at risk. Thay have corroborated the common wisdom that race, social class, single-parent families, and lack of medical care are all contributing factors. But some have also discovered that a major factor in students' lives that leads to depression, dropping out, drugs, jail, and suicide appears to be the school experience itself: ability groups, grade retention, college pressures, working alone, denial of strengths and focus on weaknesses, and an information-rich, experience-poor curriculum that students must endure and frequently ignore. All of this suggests to me that we educators are a major part of the problem rather than merely the helpless victims of cultural circumstances. Maybe schools, too, would benefit by adhering to the medical edict: first, do no harm.

Perhaps the most powerful asset of the school-based reformer is moral outrage. How often do you hear yourself saying, "Dammit, I'm not going to keep putting all of these African American and Hispanic kids in the bottom ability group!" "Sit 'n' git is no longer acceptable." How much of your energy are you expending in school to help others accept the unacceptable? How much energy trying to *change* the unacceptable?

What do you think? Do you believe that the problems of schools and the profound transformations in our society and in our students are sufficient to require equally profound changes in what you do in your school?

Question 5: How Can You Build a High-Performing School Improvement Team from a Cast of Bright, Stubborn, Willful, Idiosyncratic Goats—or from a Herd of Sheep?

All restructuring efforts I know are based on the assumption that serious change will come only from a collective effort—for example, a school team, a school improvement council—that stimulates, envisions, observes, plans, implements, and monitors change. In Chicago, for instance, every school has a school leadership team consisting of two teachers, six parents, two community members, and the principal. Yet, as we all know, putting two teachers, six parents, two community members, and a principal around a table does not a team make. It makes two teacher, six parents, two community members, and a principal. Through what alchemy is a disparate (sometimes desperate) group of individuals, each accustomed to having it his or her own way in a small domain—say, behind the door of an algebra classroom—going to learn to work together in the best interests of the larger domain?

As the Rhode Island teacher leaders testify, the formation of a high-performing school team requires developing group process skills in running effective meetings, in consensus building within the team and within the school, in securing and utilizing resources, and in developing action plans and evaluating outcomes. A precondition for successful reform is interdependence. You must want to work together; that is, you must have the will. And you must know how to work together; that is, you must have the skill. Yet most of us in schools are not very good at collaborating, and never have been. God did not create self-contained classrooms, university departments, and isolated schools within a district. We did, because we find working alone easier and safer than working together.

Personal change must precede and accompany a collective change. Can we work together? Do we even *want* to? What makes us think that under the banner of reform we will work together any better than we have in the past? By what means is an assortment of willful individuals in your school going to become a team? Can goats work together without becoming sheep? Or is the phrase *school improvement team* another oxymoron of the times, along with jumbo shrimp?

We educators can take heart from the words of Benjamin Franklin at the final session of the Constitutional Convention in Philadelphia, that hot summer of 1787: "When you assemble a number of men, to have the advantage of their joint wisdom, you inevitably assemble with those men all their prejudices, their passions, their errors of opinion, their local interests, and their selfish views. From such an assembly can a *perfect* production be expected?" The founding fathers, working together, came up with a pretty reputable document: the Constitution of the United States. It can be done.

Question 6: How Much Reform Is Enough?

This question arises as more schools engage in self-renewal. Is adopting a shopping center enough, or should we do more? We've created a school improvement council. We've shown that we can do it. Now can we get on with our business? How far should we go? Where is the line between an oil change and a major overhaul, between tinkering and reform, between reform and revolution, and between revolution and revulsion? How do we know when we're there?

I recently went to get my car inspected. The woman ahead of me asked her young son to go back and look at the taillights as she flicked the turn signal lever. As he studied the dusty lenses, the child yelled to his mother, "It's working; it's not working; it's working; it's not working."

How far do we go in the name of reform? I think we go until it is working—not intermittently, but most of the time—for students, teachers, administrators, and parents. That is, we go until life in the schoolhouse becomes more the solution than the problem for all its occupants. We're not there until the organization we call *school* becomes just as agile, adept, and persistent at changing as the needs, situations, and characteristics of those who live under its roof. By this criterion, we will probably *never* "get there," for reform, of course, is not an end in itself; it is a means to help us work better together for our own and for our students' benefit.

So, how much reform is enough—in *your* schoolhouse?

Question 7: What About Your School Needs to be Reformed?

Most critics value some qualities of schools and abhor others. Few reformers propose to throw the baby out with the bathwater. Each has a different prescription, however. For some, learning outcomes need to be defined more precisely. For others, it's all about test scores. Still others want better preparation of students for the job market. Multiple action plans are swamping and defeating attempts to reform schools. As anyone who works in schools knows, you can move on only a few important fronts at once. Which shall they be? What about your school most needs to be improved?

Because the world outside and the students inside are changing so fast and in such unpredictable ways, the most important change to bring to the schoolhouse is a culture of continual adaptability, experimentation, and invention. Every school can become a lab school stocked with philosophers who can look with new eyes and who can constantly ask, Why? Why are the older students upstairs and the younger ones down? Why do teachers talk 85 percent of the time, and students talk 15 percent of the time, when students outnumber teachers twenty-eight to one? Why are adults teaching young people about computers when many young people know more about computers than most adults? Why?

We need to scrutinize—not every ten years for accreditation but every day—the systemic conditions that enrich and those that assault students and adults. The continual invention of new ways must replace perpetuation of comfortable routine or even the enshrinement of new ideas.

We must not bolt reform to the floor, otherwise we merely replace old, encrusted ways of doing things with new practices that will soon become old and encrusted. Schools can become places where everything is written in chalk, not engraved in stone, where thinking and practice are tentative until more promising thinking and practice emerge. For this change to occur, school people must exercise some higher-order thinking skills and enlist help from the left-brained, the right-brained, and maybe even the harebrained. Most of all, we need to spend less time trying to help others accept the unacceptable and more time trying to change the unacceptable.

So, what about your school needs to be reformed?

Question 8: Can School People Reform the Schools?

Our prominent American philosopher Yogi Berra once observed, "I can't hit and think at the same time." Well, what about you? Can you maintain an already overloaded, complex, and demanding classroom or school and *in addition* become a serious architect, designer, and engineer, dismantling one operation and substituting another? Can you invent *and* maintain? The idea of living simultaneously in an old place of fifty-five-minute periods while you are jumping to a new one of interdisciplinary units or shared leadership is very difficult.

If you are to become the new reformers of the twenty-first century, you must persist in the face of tough, tedious questions like these: Do you restructure schools with only the best and brightest teachers and principals in mind, or do you grapple with the reality of deadwood and incompetence? Do you feel that you can do more and better only with more money? Do you acknowledge the presence in schools of those who are pleased to be led as well as those who want to exert leadership? Are you who live in schools going to create policies—as those who live outside schools have done—that often insult the capable and leave the incompetent untouched?

Your job, then, is massive. You must not only strengthen confidence in yourselves and the confidence of others in you but also help those outside the schools figure out how they can best aid the efforts of those inside the schools. You have to "staff-develop" officials in state departments of education, in universities, in the federal government, and in the district office so that they will provide the kind of help you need in order to successfully improve your school. A formidable lesson plan. The question is a big one: Can you reform your school?

• • •

These are some of the tough questions that confront and trouble school-based reformers. And these are questions that trouble me as I read about and observe the call to reform our nation's schools and as I think about the possibility of schools becoming self-renewing organizations. I hope I have been successful in confronting and troubling you with them as well! In the foregoing chapters, I have attempted to supply some of my own answers. But the important answers to these questions, those on which school reform rests, are your answers, not mine.

Each of us may feel inconsequential as an agent of serious change in our school. But we can take heart and gain strength from one teacher leader, who concluded, "I draw hope from the knowledge that even a tiny insect can make its presence felt in a dramatic way to a very large animal."

14

RISK

> The trouble is, if you don't risk anything, you risk everything. —*Carl Jung*

Monday morning in school can be a dangerous time, for over the weekend, in addition to healing from the events of the previous week, teachers begin to look ahead, to plan, and to dream.

When I was teaching elementary school, a doctoral student at work on her thesis came through the school. She was interested in the little conversation—little dance, really—that takes place when a teacher comes to the principal on Monday morning with a new idea: "I want to take the kids on a field trip, on a boat around the Farallon Islands. This will culminate our study of marine biology, ecology, geology, and the California coast. In addition, I'll relate the trip to my haiku unit and our study of the early explorers. I've never done it before, but I think it will blow the kids' socks off!"

The enterprising researcher was interviewing teachers and principals about similar conversations in which they had participated. And she was observing as many of these little scenes as she could find and join.

A few months later, as agreed, she returned with her findings, which I remember to this day: she discovered that most school principals greet a teacher's expression of a desire to try something new with a very curious, very similar set of responses:

First response: worried look, hunched back, raised eyebrows, defensive posture. This is quite remarkable, when you think about it. Here is a teacher, very excited about trying something new, willing to go to great lengths to devise a more promising way of teaching youngsters, doing precisely what we hope *all* teachers will do; and the first response of the principal is a body language that connotes disapproval, fear, and defensiveness.

Second response: the principal parades a litany of reasons why this is a bad idea and can not possibly work. "The last time anyone took a field trip on the water, five kids got seasick—and I'm still hearing from the angry parents and the school board." "If I let you take this trip, how about the other fourth grades?" "But how will this fit into the district's scope and sequence?" "But we haven't got it in the budget." And, of course, "This field trip will deflect precious time and energy away from preparation for the state's standardized tests." You know the list. I know the list. I've heard the list, and as principal, I've *recited* the list!

If the heroic teacher is not yet deterred by this reception of her weekend's dream, a third predictable response from the principal awaits her: "Well, let me think it over. Get back to me in a couple of weeks." The stall. And the principal crosses his fingers and hopes the problem will go away, and he'll never see this teacher again—at least not on this subject.

But as T. E. Lawrence observed, "All men dream: but not equally. Those who dream by night in the dusty recesses of their mind wake in the day to find that it was vanity: but the dreamers of the day are dangerous men, for they may act their dream with open eyes, to make it possible."[1]

Two weeks later, undeterred, our daytime dreamer becomes a teacher leader and shows up in the principal's office again. "I've given this a lot of thought, and I'm even more convinced that this will be a super culminating activity for the class this year. It ties all the strands of our curriculum together. I can get parents involved, the other fourth grades want to participate, and we're going to conduct this as carefully as the invasion of Normandy. And I have lots of seasickness pills!"

The final response of the reluctant principal: "OK. You can go on this field trip. But remember—if anything happens, it's *your* responsibility."

A Culture of Caution

What an extraordinary series of encounters between principal and teacher. The incontrovertible message from one to the other seems to be, "Look at all the work and all the problems that promoting learning for youngsters is going to cause us." But what's even more disheartening is that the response of this principal to the teacher's wish to take the field trip is the response of *most* administrators to the initiatives of *most* teachers.

Moreover, this protocol of responses is endemic in our profession. It's what the principal hears when she approaches the superintendent about setting up an innovative program between inner-city and suburban school children at the Museum of Science. Worried look. A parade of the reasons why not. "Get back to me." "OK, but it's *your* responsibility."

And it's the set of responses that students hear when they approach the teacher with a novel idea: "Instead of writing a report on the explorers, me and Jimmy want to take a video camera out into the woods and explore them, make a film, and come back and show it to the class." Worried look. A parade of the reasons why not. "Get back to me." And so it goes.

This pattern suggests that the culture of our profession is one of pathological caution. In schools, too often we play not to lose. Everyone is behaving so as not to get a reprimand filed in their "folder." Precious few are playing to *win*. This, despite the fact that we all know what happens when the team in the final quarter plays not to lose. They *lose!*

One of the Rhode Island teacher leaders put it this way:

> It seems that when the status quo is threatened by anything new, an immediate systemic defense mechanism comes to life. Even when people appear willing to try something new, they eventually revert to the status quo.

The only good question to ask of that teacher who wants to take the field trip around the Farallon Islands (and to ask of the teacher who this May wants to do exactly what she did last May) is, "So what do you think the students will learn from this experience?" If the teacher responds with, "Well, you know, it's the last month of school, and we all need to get out," there is ample cause to question the field trip. If, however, the teacher responds with a litany of her own about the expected learning the carefully planned trip will yield, the response we'd all like to hear from the principal is, "Let's do it! Can I come along? If it doesn't work out, we'll share the responsibility."

In all too many schools and systems, of course, if one does take the risk and it doesn't work out (and frequently if it *does*), one is hung out to dry, alone at the end of the branch. Maybe we could acquire some courage and inspiration from Earl Warren, former chief justice: "Everything I did in my life that was worthwhile I caught hell for."

How Much Am I Prepared to Risk?

This brings me to one more question I would like to pose—probably the most important of all, for this is the question on which rests the promise of school-based reform: How much are you prepared to risk? How much are you prepared to risk of what is familiar, comfortable, safe, and perhaps working well for you, in the name of better education for others?

This little volume has been about risk-taking. Turning the radio dial off of "sit 'n' git" and discovering the Experiential model demands that we get out of the bleachers and onto the field. To shift from being a member of the audience to a participant is a risk of major proportions.

The characteristic most central to the three case studies we have considered is risk. As we have seen, the teachers in Rhode Island, by virtue of being teacher leaders, take enormous risks in their schools and systems. By standing up and violating the taboos against both distinguishing themselves and presuming to know what is best for others, they risk the disapprobation of principal and peer alike.

By thinking otherwise about the preparation of school principals, the Aspiring Principals' Program constitutes one huge risk. And by redefining their lives in schools around learning together, each of the aspiring principals and distinguished principals take big risks—together.

School leaders in New Jersey who have become principal learners take risks by identifying themselves not as learn*ed* but as learn*ers*. By putting on the oxygen mask of learning, they risk disclosing to the world that they don't know how and that they intend to learn how.

At the outset, I suggested conditions necessary for getting learning curves off the chart—observation of practice, conversation about practice, reflection and writing about practice, telling stories, sharing craft knowledge, and maximizing differences in order to maximize learning. Each of them invites, even demands, profound levels of risk-taking. The ultimate risk is to disclose ourselves.

To learn is to risk; to lead others toward profound levels of learning is to risk; to promote personal and organizational renewal is to risk. To create schools hospitable to human learning is to risk. In short, the career of the lifelong learner and of the school-based reformer is the life of the risk-taker.

The possibility that schools can and will reform from within rests squarely on whether and how much teachers and principals are willing to risk in the name of good education for youngsters. We educators will improve schools only when we take risks. It's as simple as that.

If our profession's prevailing response to risk is that of the principal to the teacher wishing to pursue the field trip, there is little hope. If the response is that of the second principal—who wants to know what children will learn, wants to come along, and is willing to share responsibility—there is cause for much hope indeed.

Risk-Taking and Learning

Why is a culture of risk-taking so crucial to schools of the twenty-first century? Because human learning is most profound, most transformative, and most enduring when two conditions are present: when we take risks and when a safety strap or belaying line supports us when we fall, so that we don't get killed.

Failure is often far less painful and debilitating than the *fear* of failure. More important for educators, there is growth and learning in failure. There is no growth and no learning in fear of failure. If you take away a person's right to fail, you take away her right to succeed. Schools are about growth, learning—and success. A failure experience becomes an especially good teacher when accompanied by observation, reflection, conversation, and efforts to make sense of the failure: So what happened? What did you learn from the experience? If you had it to do over again, how would you do it differently? How might you get help?

Schools exist to promote and sustain profound levels of human learning. Yet neither of the two conditions perhaps most closely associated with human learning—risk-taking and a safety strap for those who risk—are present in schools. These conditions are interdependent and at the very core of a culture hospitable to human learning.

A refreshing few educators see the connection between leading, learning, and risk-taking. They are working to build school cultures in which the presence of safety lines encourages risk-taking and even the creation of communities of risk-takers. For example, the school system of Appleton, Wisconsin, after lengthy conversations, came to a vision. One of its central elements was the importance of risk-taking within the system, within each school, and within each classroom. Risk-taking became embedded in the culture of the entire school system. Ready to "walk the talk," the educators in Appleton printed off and distributed to central office administrators, principals, teachers, parents, and students hundreds of little cards, on each of which was printed these words: "*I blew it.* I tried something new and innovative, and it didn't work as well as I wanted. This coupon entitles me to be free of criticism for my efforts. I'll continue to pursue ways to help our district be successful." What a powerful safety strap! And what a wonderful invitation to risk. And to learn.

I remember coming into a middle school in another district and being welcomed by these words, emblazoned on the wall of the front hall: "Anything worth doing is worth doing badly—at first"—another safety strap that gives all members of the school community permission to risk. In the principal's office of yet another school, I saw these words: "Throughout history the most common, debilitating human condition has been cold feet."

It *is* possible to transform a culture of caution into one that not only tolerates but also expects, rewards, even celebrates risk-taking. There *is* a repertoire of means. In such a culture, the school is always improving, and the youngsters and adults are always learning.

Take a Risk

For the teacher or administrator who would make risk-taking a discussable and embed this quality in the life of the community of learners, I offer the little questionnaire in Exhibit 14.1 to distribute—and to learn from. Teachers give it to students, principals to teachers, teachers and administrators to parents, and superintendents to the school-based educators.

It is a risk, of course, even to hand out this questionnaire, and especially to ask and learn how those around us experience us as risk-takers. Yet there is no more important lens through which the educator who would promote human learning and school reform can examine himself. Try it. Versions of this instrument could be developed and administered to different populations

Please check the one that applies most.

I see you as

- ______ Very timid—not a risk-taker.
- ______ Cautious, one who occasionally takes calculated risks.
- ______ One who frequently takes risks that promote someone's learning.
- ______ One who is always ready to take a risk if it might improve the quality of students' or adults' learning or the quality of the school.

Exhibit 14.1. Risk-Taking Assessment

with whom we work. And it could be self-administered. Some of the cautious may be perceived as bold, and some who consider themselves courageous risk-takers may learn that this is not how the world sees them. The educator who wishes to build a school culture in which risk-taking is prominent can exercise no greater influence than by taking risks himself.

Consider one of Aesop's fables. Once upon a time, a number of mice called a meeting to decide the best means of ridding themselves of a cat that had killed a great number of their friends and relations. Various plans were discussed and rejected, until at last a young mouse came forward and proposed that a bell should be hung round the tyrant's neck, that they might, in the future, have warning of her movements and be able to escape.

The suggestion was received joyfully by nearly all, but an old mouse, who had sat silent for some time, got up and said, "While I consider the plan to be a very clever one and feel sure that it would prove to be quite successful if carried out, I would like to know who is going to bell the cat?"

Like belling the cat, reforming schools is not for the faint-hearted. *Risk-free change* is an oxymoron. Change is always accompanied by risk. Indeed, the ideograph from the Chinese language that represents *opportunity* is the very same symbol as that which represents *danger*. They go hand in hand. The ancient Chinese believed that when you approached danger, you must not turn back, for an opportunity was clearly nearby. Similarly, when a new opportunity presents itself, it's important to know that dangers abound.

One principal, faced with impending restructuring, perceptively described to me his conflicting feelings about change:

> I feel like a bird that has been caged by rules and regulations for a long time. With school reform, the door is now open. I'm standing at the edge. Will I dare to fly out? I am beginning to realize that the bars of the cage that have imprisoned me all these years have been the very same bars that have protected me from the hawks and falcons out there. I'm not sure I'm going to fly.

Schools are cautious and confusing cages where teachers, principals, and students try to create pockets of safety and sanity for themselves, reluctant to leave these safe quarters for parts unknown. Schools are also storehouses of our memories. To radically transform them is not simply risky; doing so can feel like institutional homicide. Can we reform something to which we have been for so long deeply attached? Do we want to? Altering the way we have always done things carries costs of not only risk and failure but also sadness and loss. In order to change and move to the new, we must accept and grieve the loss of the old.

So the toughest question for you who would reform your schools remains: Just how much are you prepared to risk of what is familiar, comfortable, and safe for you in the name of better education for others?

The trouble is, if you don't risk anything, you risk everything.

15

COMING TO A VISION

> Your work is to discover your work—and to give your heart to it. —*Buddha*

Here in Maine there are two classes of citizens: the native residents who have farmed and fished these bony fields and waters for generations, and the rest of us—the nonresidents, the summer people, the rusticators. Alas, even after sixty-three years of part-time residence I am still "from away."

So it is in schools: there are the resident natives of the schoolhouse who live and toil there each day for hour upon hour. And then there are the "tourists" who come from universities, central offices, and state departments to visit. As in Maine, no number of these visits will ever transform the tourist into the native.

I'm a school junkie. I like to visit schools. Lots of them. Unfortunately, I seldom spend much time in a single school. I admit it: unlike the years when I worked in schools, I'm now a tourist, not a resident. I call my brief visits to schools my "teabag through the bathtub" school of social science.

Nonetheless, in order to learn as much as I can about the essence of a school in but a few hours, I like to arrive equipped with a straightforward, nonthreatening, engaging question. I find having but one question yields richer observation, conversation, and learning than having 101 questions. I try to be respectful asking my question and listening to the response from teachers, parents, students, or administrators. If I can identify a generative, yeasty question, I find that even in an hour or two, a school will turn over the keys to the store and reveal its innermost secrets.

For a few years I was captured by the question, Can you tell me how students are assigned to teachers each year? How the decision is made about which pupil will be instructed by which adult is a most revealing and, as parents know, a most consequential question.

School Vision

Lately I've come to unfamiliar schools with a different question. The conversation typically proceeds along this path:

Roland: Does your school have a vision?
Teacher: Oh, yes.
Roland: Could you tell me what it is?
Teacher: I can't get all of the words straight . . . they have it down at the office.
Roland: How did your school come to have this vision?
Teacher: There was a committee that met for several months last spring and came up with it.
Roland: Do you think this vision is having much influence on everyone's behavior around here?
Teacher: Probably a little.

Think about it. When next you visit an unfamiliar school (or even your own!), try asking, "Do you know your school's vision? How did your school come to have this vision?" The responses you hear may take very different, possibly more hopeful directions. In any case, each response discloses important qualities of the school's essence.

There is no more important work for school-based reformers than helping create and then employing an inspiring, useful vision. The capacity to create purposeful reform rests with the capacity of educators to create an authentic vision for their school. For as Chekhov wrote, "If you cry 'forward' you must without fail make plans in what direction to go."

"Every school must have a vision." This, as we have seen, is a message delivered to teachers, students, parents, and principals in schools from rural Alaska to the urban Bronx. For example, the United States Department of Education awards blue ribbon school status to schools with "a clear vision and sense of mission that is shared by all connected with the school." The state of Connecticut certifies only principals and superintendents who demonstrate "the ability to develop and articulate a vision of excellence in teaching and learning."

A widespread realization seems to have come over our profession that every school should have a compelling, shared conception of what the school should become. The underlying logic appears to be simple and straightforward: a school with a vigorous, soaring vision of what it might become is more likely to become that; without a vision, a school is unlikely to improve. Therefore, every school should have one.

This is simple to say, perhaps, but immensely complicated to achieve. I find the enterprise of making visions for schools to be at once hopeful and exciting yet imperiled by a host of seldom-asked and inadequately addressed questions. Keeping your school's vision in mind, let's consider these questions:

Just what is a school vision? The word *vision* derives from the Latin verb *videre*, which means "to see." What does your vision help us see? Is it a holiday shopping list, a collection of isolated characteristics deemed to be desirable? Is it a coherent, logically connected set of beliefs? What is the difference between a vision, a mission, a philosophy, and the familiar, often tired educational concept of "goals and objectives"?

Why is it important that your school have a vision? What advantages come to individuals and to schools that have a vision? Are there any *dis*advantages associated with your school's vision? What's the difference between a personal vision and a collective vision?

Where does your personal vision come from? Your own early experience in school? Your parents? From reading the literature? From what you want for youngsters? From what you believe about the conditions for learning? From what you believe is a vibrant workplace for adults?

When you look for a school vision, where do you find it? Is your personal vision reflected in your school vision?

Who are the individuals best qualified to offer vision to schools? National politicians? The members of the business world? University people? School administrators? The central office? Teachers? Parents? Students? How inclusive should (or can) the vision-making process be? Can youngsters in your school become visionaries?

Can you have confidence that a school organized around and driven by the visions of school practitioners will result in a better and more humane learning environment for youngsters and adults than we have seen in schools dominated by external visions?

Is whatever vision your school comes up with acceptable? Or are some visions better than others? What are the characteristics of a "good" vision? What criteria might we employ to assess your school's vision?

Will a "good" vision in and of itself enlist an enthusiastic and voluntary following?

How do you get everyone to "buy in" to a vision?

What is the relationship between your personal vision and the collective vision you see at your school? Would you like the fit to be congruent? Or are there some advantages for a school and for teachers and administrators when personal visions do not coincide completely with the school's vision?

Once specified, are visions permanent? Or are they organic? If visions always change, should your school engrave its vision in granite over the schoolhouse door, or should it be expressed in pencil or chalk, acknowledging a process of continual refinement and updating?

Can your school's vision ever be fully realized? Or does it provide more of a sense of direction, like a compass or the North Star? Can you ever get to "north"?

What evidence would you accept that your school's vision is being achieved? Or is it sufficient that a vision be approached incrementally?

If visions are such good things, why have they been so rare in the history of schools?

What are the vision killers in your school that lurk like toxic viruses? "They'll never let us" and "What are we supposed to do"? How can we extinguish these vision killers?

Should all schools within a district have identical visions? Should they have similar visions? Should they have unique visions?

What is the difference between, on the one hand, a vision statement that is window dressing, seldom referred to and likely to collect dust in the principal's office along with those old curriculum guides, and, on the other hand, a compelling vision in which all members of the school community are deeply and personally invested? How do you avoid the former and develop the latter?

Different Routes to a Vision

These, then, are some of the questions that accompany the task of creating a school vision. They are among the issues badly in need of explication and exploration if schools are to develop more than a primitive, inert window dressing. There are many more questions, of course. They suggest that developing a school vision is a far more complicated, sophisticated, and perilous activity than many suspect. Vision making hardly lends itself to tidy resolution during a two-hour faculty meeting.

But there is yet another question I would like to address here: How does a school come to have a vision? States mandate that every school will have a vision or a mission statement. I find a curious confidence in our profession, that if we expect and require a school to have a vision, it will have one. A big step is missing: the process. By what means will a school that has lived quite happily (or unhappily) with little or no vision come to have one? The process may be self-evident to some; it certainly isn't to me.

In the past few years, I have enjoyed visiting a number of schools with visions and many more struggling to develop them. I ask, "How is it that this school has come or is coming to have a vision?" I find the conversation that follows from this question to be an unusually rich, reflective, and revealing one. Schools report many paths toward a school vision, each with clear advantages and disadvantages. Let me share this craft knowledge that has been shared with me.

Inherit a Vision

Many schools—venerable New England preparatory schools, for instance—were founded with the driving vision of a driving visionary. Strong remnants of the original vision endure. A new teacher or headmaster is chosen because of her adherence to this vision. The vision perpetuates itself from one generation to the next as suggested by the words of one headmaster: "We have a clear framework within which to live and conduct our lives together. We have a ready-made role model, worthy of emulation, a goal to seek, a vision of what life should be." The vision was there in 1870; it's still there.

An advantage to inheriting a vision is that school people don't need to go through the periodic, introspective turmoil of crafting a vision. A disadvantage is that the vision was engraved in the granite of the past, whereas the faculty come from the present and the students must be prepared for the future. Granite does not lend itself to easy adaptation. Harvard president Charles William Eliot put it this way in his inaugural address: "A good past is positively dangerous if it makes us content with the present and so unprepared for the future."

Explicate a Vision

Many schools live with an implicit vision. No one has ever gone to the trouble of putting into writing "what we believe in around here." But a vision nonetheless permeates the day-to-day activities of the school. These schools are coming to have a vision by making overt what has been covert. They ask the questions, What have we been doing? What is important to us in the school? Do we like what we see?

An advantage of this method is that the vision is comfortable, genuine, and already existing. What is new is the language into which past action is now encoded. A disadvantage may be that these schools reify what they have been doing, rather than ask, What would we like to do in the future? Another disadvantage is that waking a sleeping baby often causes noise. When I was a principal, I found that there were times when it was better not to attempt to make the covert overt.

Refine a Vision

Many schools are developing new visions by taking inventory of past practice and present aspirations, then tuning them up for the twenty-first century. They may introduce computer technology into the curriculum. They may insert a line about preparing students for a competitive, international workplace. These schools combine the best of the past with the promises and demands of the future, updating what they feel is basically a sound program, pedagogy, and existing vision.

The advantage of this pragmatic method of vision making is that there is something in it for everyone—school people, critics, and children. A disadvantage may be that this becomes an exercise in putting new patches on a defective tire. An incremental approach leads more often to tinkering, seldom to reform, and almost never to the fundamental "restructuring" in which schools these days are being called on to engage.

Borrow a Vision

Teachers and principals have long lived with meager resources. School people are used to scrounging for desks, globes, and masking tape. The same skills are useful in creating a vision. Junior high faculty members charged with becoming a middle school might visit a dozen middle schools with perfectly good visions and bring back pieces of middle school language, practice, and philosophy that they particularly like. Then they assemble these pieces into their unique "Thomas Jefferson Middle School Vision."

A clear advantage to this method is the acknowledgment of the treasure trove of rich craft knowledge and expertise of other educators that awaits anyone persistent enough to ferret it out. A disadvantage may be that this pieced-together vision may be more of a collage than a vision with strong, coherent core values to which every practice is related.

Buy a Vision

Out there on the market is an impressive variety of "visions" for a good school. A school can literally buy the "Comer model," the "Copernican Plan," the "Paidea Proposal," or the "effective schools" approach. Indeed, schools in Memphis are expected to select—from among approved alternatives—a vision around which the school will be organized and run. Consultants then come to the school and deliver their visions and accompanying practices, along with workshops and staff development activities, all of which will ensure that *their* vision will be more or less faithfully transplanted to the school.

An advantage of this method is that most of these conceptions are indeed rich, coherent, and fundamentally different from business as usual. A further advantage within the school is that if members of the faculty don't like the new Paidea vision, they can shoot at Mortimer Adler, not at one another. A disadvantage may be that looking outside for a vision reinforces the belief that those who live underneath the roof of the schoolhouse are unable to get their own house in order, thereby perpetuating the helplessness and dependency that is so evident at all levels in our profession.

Inflict a Vision

One of the most common means whereby schools report they have come to a vision is by having a person or an office outside the building supply that vision. A superintendent might say to principals, "Your schools don't have visions. Here's what we believe in this system; here's what you will believe in each of your schools." The principal, in turn, inflicts this vision on the teachers, who inflict it on the students. Of course, these days this kind of educational imperialism is camouflaged with proper "involvement" and "committees," but underneath, everyone knows what is going on.

An advantage of this approach is that such a vision can come to a school quickly and be uniformly and impressively portrayed (if not practiced) throughout the district. Uniformity suggests that we know what we are doing here. Disadvantages of course are that teachers and principals are gifted and talented at offering superficial compliance to an imposed ideology while at the same time thwarting it or keeping two sets of books. This leads all too often to what one teacher called the kidney stone school of reform: painful at first, but this too shall pass. As Frank Lloyd Wright advised us, "Beware of building from the top down."

Hire a Vision

As we know, in the last few decades the world has rediscovered the central place of the school principal in promoting—or subverting—school improvement. When a school is adrift and rudderless, all hands blame the captain. A common practice is to fire (or transfer) the nonperforming principal and mount an intergalactic search for an "educational leader." Of each candidate, the question now asked is, What is your vision of a good school? When the selection committee, superintendent, and board hear the vision they like, they hire the candidate. The implicit understanding is that by June, the floundering school will have come to resemble the new principal's vision.

An advantage of this approach is that a change in leadership may well usher fundamental change into a school, and the fresh, new vision may eventually be reflected in the school's culture. Of concern is the assumption that the proper creator and purveyor of vision is the principal: "My vision is our vision; yours is negotiable." The responsibility of others is to receive, celebrate, and fulfill the principal's vision. Another disadvantage is that the principal, hired with the mandate to bring his or her vision to the troubled school, will inflict it, again sustaining the paternalism—"It's the principal's school, not ours"—that has been all too prevalent in the past. Unfortunately, as we have noted, the knight riding on a white horse into the fray to rescue the troubled masses doesn't work very well these days.

Homogenize a Vision

A practice by means of which some schools report they come to have visions is to invite members of the major constituencies to reveal their personal visions. Teachers, parents, administrators, and perhaps students individually submit their conceptions of an ideal school. Each contributes his or her most cherished beliefs and practices. Then, through some form of content analysis, a search is mounted for common elements: "Before we leave here at four-thirty today, we will have a statement we can all agree on." These common elements then become the school's vision.

An advantage of this method is that there is little in the final vision that was not in the vision of each contributor—and little that is unfamiliar or threatening. There should be no conflict, no resistance, no naysayers. We can assume all will embrace this common vision.

One disadvantage is that people will feel that "there was much in my personal vision that I don't see reflected in this collective vision. I feel my hands and feet have been cut off. I no longer have much interest in this school vision because I don't see me in it."

More important, the least common denominator tends to exclude out-of-the-box thinking—the fresh, inventive, and often most promising ideas held by only one or two individuals. The homogenized vision is one whose sharp edges have been dulled. It is indeed a *least* common denominator. Finally, homogenized visions tend to be random collections of apple pie bromides with no organizing principle or backbone: "We care for the individual child."

Grow a Vision

Thus far, I have suggested a repertoire of different paths by means of which schools come to have visions. Combinations of these are common. There are many ways a school can come to have a vision; each offers advantages and disadvantages, and each generates a different kind of final product with different ripple effects in practice. Given the mandate that a school must have a vision, it is not self-evident just how that school will come to a vision, or even that it will. The fuzzy and crucial art of vision making is badly in need of clarification. A school must make deliberate choices not only to have a vision and about what that vision shall be but also of the means by which it intends to craft the vision.

Let me share my bias here. The few schools I visit that have a vital, courageous, demanding, uplifting vision—where most educators and students are familiar with the vision, where day-to-day behavior is constantly scrutinized for evidence of congruity with that vision, and where the school is incrementally approaching that vision—are schools where school-based educators have succeeded in *growing* their own vision. That is, by some form of hydroponics, agriculture, or alchemy, members of the school community—perhaps but not always led by the principal—devise a process for examining their school, looking at what the school is and isn't doing for little people and big people. Then, together, they wonder; they contemplate possible and desirable futures; and through some means, they create together a vision that provides a new and profound sense of purpose for the organization and for each of its members. Through this process, the group extracts from its members not their commonalties but the gold nuggets that offer the most promising ideas.

A vision is a kind of moral imagination that gives school people, individually and collectively, the ability to see their school not only as it is but also as they would like it to become. It is an overall conception of what educators want their school to stand for, a map revealing how all the parts fit together and, above all, just how the vision of each individual is related to the collective vision of the organization.

A precondition for constructing an authentic, collective vision is that each school educator must come to grips with his or her own personal vision. Not only are we each entitled to our own conception of a good school; each of us as an educator *must* have our own conception of a good school—and make it accessible to our colleagues.

A school's vision must then somehow emerge from the primal ooze of these many personal visions; otherwise, the collective vision will be lifeless: The inhabitants of the schoolhouse may comply with the school's vision, but they will not commit to it.

There are many advantages of a homegrown vision. It enlists and reflects not the common thinking but the *best* thinking, beliefs, ideals, and ideas of the entire school community. If the process is inclusive and genuine, the vision is likely to be embracing and honest. Those who have felt empowered as architects, engineers, and designers are likely to feel empowered as builders. Yet few school communities of which I am aware have successfully devised a process that provides the fertile soil in which a vision can grow and flourish. School cultures, all too often barren, suspicious, and characterized by isolation, cannot grow a plant as delicate and yet as deeply rooted as a vision. Before it can support new life, the soil must be enriched.

My good friend David Hagstrom, former principal of the Denali Elementary School in Fairbanks, Alaska, tells this remarkable story about growing a vision:

> I asked some parents, "What do you folks want for your children, here at the school?" Fortunately, I was pretty patient regarding "wait time." This was good, because the four of them just stared at me in silence—for a really long time. Finally, one of the parents spoke: "You know, no one has ever asked us a question like that, but if you can handle the truth, I'm going to answer the question." She went on to explain that her two children really appreciated living in Fairbanks. "It's a real outdoors kind of place, and my kids enjoy building forts along the river in the summertime and snow houses in the winter. They can be true adventurers in their free time," she declared. "But then they enter this dark, dank school, and there's not a hint of that exploring fun that gets them so excited. This is really a pretty dreary place for children. I want my children to be the same kind of explorers inside the school as they are outside. I'd like school to be an exciting experience for them."
>
> On hearing this, another parent agreed enthusiastically: "You sure got that one right! But there's something else I'd like for my children, here at this school. Somehow I'd like the school to teach the concept of giving, not taking. What I mean is: for years and years, outsiders have been taking from Alaska. Fishing folks come up from Washington State and take the fish out. Forest products people come in and take the wood out. Gold miners used to take the gold out. And, of course, the oil tankers take the oil out. To add insult to injury, now, in the process of taking out the oil, Exxon has spilled oil all across some of the most pristine beauty of Alaska! It's simply ridiculous! And because it's so ridiculous, I want my kids to learn to be givers, not takers."
>
> The hallway conversation went on in this way for about two hours. At the end of the time, I was really quite energized, and so

I said, "This has been good. Do we want to continue this talk at another time?" In response, everyone indicated the need to continue the conversation, and, after a rather frustrating attempt to figure out a "next time," the parent who had initiated the initial response extended this invitation: "Here's an offer you can't resist. I'll make breakfast next Tuesday morning if you'll all come. What are you all doing at six next Tuesday? I can't imagine that you've got a lot scheduled at that hour." We all laughed, as she continued, "So be at my house at six in the morning; we'll live with this question some more, and we'll talk."

Well, we were, and we did. We were there, and we continued to live in the question, What do we want for our children, here in this school? Interestingly, the answers given in the hallway remained steadily the same. At the conclusion of the breakfast meeting, the people in Sue's kitchen strongly indicated that they wanted the children to be explorers—maybe even discoverers—and givers, not takers. So as we were about to part company that morning, I asked: "Shall we meet again?" It was quite clear that the group wanted to meet again, so with a gleam in her eyes, Sue issued a new invitation: "Come on back next Tuesday, at the same time. But here's the deal: each one of us has to bring someone. It doesn't matter whether it's a teacher, parent, child, or neighbor. You all have to bring someone—as your ticket to eat. Then, with ten of us, let's see if others have different answers to the question that's before us. See you next week with a child, friend, or colleague. Remember, be here at six!"

And we were there the following week at six. And the following week, and for many weeks thereafter. As the months went by, the breakfast become a potluck, and our numbers swelled. The question remained the same . . . as did the answers. *What do we want for our children here in this school? We want them to become explorers—and givers, not takers*. Soon it became clear that what we wanted to create was a math and science magnet school with a strong character component that stressed the importance of service to the community.

Over the following year, the entire school community became involved, enlisted the aid of the science department faculty at the University of Alaska, engaged the support of the Alaska Department of Education, and mobilized the entire neighborhood that surrounded the school. Parents became teachers, children became discoverers, and I—the "substitute principal"—became totally caught up in the adventure of it all. Where earlier I had been exhausted, I was now amazed and invigorated. As the adventure grew exponentially before my eyes, I dismissed all the academic pronouncements I'd been used to sharing with my students at the university. Instead, I recalled (and endorsed) words that the theologian, Henri Nouwen, shared with me years ago: "Lose yourself in the work of the group, David, and then find yourself again, revitalizing the group." Without a doubt, I had lost myself in the work of these children, teachers, parents, and neighbors. They—*we all*—had become like eager little kids discovering things together for the very first time. As we went about our work of learning earth science ideas, the laws of physics, and Alaska Native ways of understanding the world, we were becoming a learning community, and we were coming to strongly value the contributions of each and every human being in our midst.

The Denali staff elected from that time forward to . . . find out what (children, parents, and neighbors) were passionate about, and then pour it on. This can become our mission, they felt. "This is how we will honor our people."

So this is how we worked. And, as we honored each person for who they were and what they offered, we truly became "one people." We had become united around a wish to provide a wonderful education for our children, and in that uniting we had identified the contributions that each of us could make that would make that wish come true. As I reflect upon our journey toward becoming the school that we wanted, I realize that we (each of us) had become the persons we had all wanted to be. And, in that process, of course, we had become the "people" (the community) we had always wanted to be.[1]

In the final analysis, growing a vision, as the Denali Elementary School community did, is among the most promising means for a school to come to a vision and the one that may yield the richest vision and most promising changes in practice. Yet it is probably the most difficult. It requires a huge amount of courage, skill, and heart. There is no packaged lesson plan, no "teacher-proof" way. It must come from within each educator and from within each school community.

In the process of coming to real visions, schools generate extraordinary new energy, good ideas, and hope. And there are no qualities more desperately needed in these days of reforming our schools than energy, good ideas, and hope. That is reason enough to engage and persist in the struggle toward an authentic school vision.

EPILOGUE

If you want to predict the future, create it.

—*Peter Drucker*

My odometer has recently made the big revolution from 1999 to 2000, and I find myself looking both back and ahead. Those of us whose careers have been dedicated to the development of youngsters, adults, and schools are asking, What will schools of the twenty-first century to be like? What would we *like* schools of the twenty-first century to be like? Sometimes, the best way to look forward is first to look backward.

In the 1940s, I attended, along with a couple dozen other scruffy rural scholars, the one-room schoolhouse at Puddle Dock in Alna, Maine, where students from grades one to eight were educated. Portions of this experience I remember well; others have happily been forgotten, perhaps repressed.

After packing up our dinner buckets, my brother, sister, and I marched, without enthusiasm, the half-mile to the end of Nelson Road. The tiny twenty-passenger yellow school bus arrived, unfortunately, on schedule. At the wheel sat Bill Humason, a slight, soft-spoken gentleman with a twinkle in his eye, who lived in and maintained a wonderful little truck garden in Alna Center.

About amidships on the same vehicle, riding shotgun, resided the ominous hulk of Suzie Humason, Bill's wife. It was her job—her pleasure—to ensure complete silence on the bus, a duty she fulfilled with distinction and intimidation. There was fire, not a twinkle, in Suzie's eye. I remember concluding what I thought was a carefully concealed, whispered conversation with my assigned seat mate, only to be severely cuffed about the head and shoulders by a blunt instrument—Suzie's fist—quickly followed by a withering glare.

Once at school, the boys entered and departed through the right-hand door, the girls by the left. (For the boys, it was good sport to see if you could use the wrong portal and get away with it.) Once inside, we were warmed by a potbellied stove, which did a good job keeping the teacher and the students at the front warm. Perhaps this is why some of us misbehaved so frequently—so we would be reseated forward. The teacher's cold glower was small price to pay for the stove's warm glow.

We scholars quenched our thirsts at a bucket of spring water at the back corner, from which we drank with a common dipper—one at a time, with permission, of course (the request signaled by one hand raised). Occasionally a foreign object found its way into the bucket—a frog, for instance—strikingly similar to the one I had seen on the way to school.

Beside the bucket were two doors leading to separate sections of the same outhouse. Permission was usually gained if two hands were waved with sufficient urgency. Inside the privy, privacy between the boys' and girls' sections was assured by a knotty partition, occasionally breached by naughty boys. This sport prevailed only when the teacher lost track of the number of students to whom she had given permission to use the outhouse.

Lessons began with the youngest students, who sat in a row at the left. When the teacher had completed perhaps ten minutes of reading instruction with that group, she moved to the next row, then the next, and so on, until, mercifully, she reached the oldest youngsters at the right side. I don't know if *she* felt relieved, but I know I did! Whereupon, back to the left she went for another sweep in handwriting, then another in . . .

Those of us who found listening to these incessant lessons tedious, boring, or impossible managed to indicate this in a variety of covert and occasionally quite overt ways. When we injected into our diction some barroom swears, out came the Lava soap. Once I was commanded to hold my unruly friend Leon while his mouth was cleansed by the diminutive teacher, whereupon it became his turn to restrain me for my oral hygiene. The lingering taste of this treatment usually served to keep our insults to the teacher, or to one another, in check for a day or two.

When the effectiveness of the Lava soap washed away, an array of switches and sticks waited behind the door in the boys' entryway. Democracy prevailed here. The teacher allowed us to select which it would be: a willow switch, an alder rod, or a stout oak stick. We usually preferred the dull stick; we found that in the hands of the weak teacher, it could do less damage than the sting of the sharp switch or the alder rod. On one occasion, the teacher went to the arsenal and was chagrined to discover that all the sticks, rods, and switches had inexplicably disappeared.

Recesses were all too infrequent and brief. We were confined to a simple swing set at which the boys and girls bantered and teased. There was quite a bit of loose gravel about, however, which afforded good ammunition. When we succeeded in hitting the bell atop the school, the teacher stormed out of the building looking for (and never finding) the perpetrator responsible for the lovely, sought-after tones. This was the best of all recess games.

Lunch was taken in the schoolyard, rain or shine. We were allowed perhaps a precious fifteen minutes to take inventory of one another's dinner boxes, effect our exchanges of peanut butter for tuna fish, and belt them down. Thence back to the arithmetic and another sweep across the room.

Finally, at precisely three o'clock, the teacher (this time) rang the schoolhouse bell. The girls were allowed a safe exit first, before the boys exploded out of the confining container. Thence immediately onto another confining container, superintended by Ms. Humason. As each of us exited the bus, appropriate hand signals were the customary punctuation with which to end the school day.

Somehow we all emerged from the tortured minutes and days of fear, boredom, and routine sufficiently educated to be promoted to another year of the same. Ah yes, that which does not destroy us makes us stronger.

My mother assured me that each day and each year I endured at the Puddle Dock school was "character building." I agree with her. Yet, to this day, I'm not sure just what was the character built.

My years of servitude at the Puddle Dock School have provided a solid reference point. During my subsequent career on the other side of the desk, as teacher, principal, and professor, I have mused at the complaints of today's students about the cafeteria food, the "mean" teacher, the problems on the bus, the workload, and the too-cold classroom.

I learned a great deal during my years attending this one-room schoolhouse, and the experience continues to generate new learnings. For instance,

- Smallness does not inevitably bring with it a culture of intimacy hospitable to learning.
- A sense of community can exist because of fear and oppression.
- Teacher leadership comes in many guises.
- Communities of learning can take peculiar forms.
- The "good old days" weren't all good. Neither were they all bad.

How much has changed? Today, I remind myself that life at the Puddle Dock School in the 1940s probably bears as much resemblance to schools of the new millennium as today's schools will resemble schools a few decades hence. In a few years, observers of our present-day schools will find them just as quaint, archaic—even arcane—as we may find Puddle Dock. Indeed, many observers *already* find them this way! To be sure, all these attempts at formal education will continue to have much in common: a curriculum, teachers, learners, places for learning. Yet other characteristics will certainly differ: rewards and punishments, physical facilities, instructional equipment, grouping of youngsters, what

students are supposed to learn, the nature of that learning, the role of the teacher and of the school leader.

It is difficult to foresee what the schools of the new millennium will look like. Many of our schools seem en route to becoming a hybrid of a nineteenth-century factory, a twentieth-century minimum security penal colony, and a twenty-first-century Educational Testing Service.

I prefer a very different future. If you want to predict the future, create it! This is precisely what school people now have the opportunity—and the imperative—to do. We must transform contemporary versions of the Puddle Dock School into learning environments worthy of the new millennium—and of the youngsters and adults who dwell in them. There is no more important work.

May this little volume help you discover your work—and give your heart to it.

APPENDIX A: A LETTER TO PARENTS

Recently, the director of the New Mission High School, David R. Perrigo, handed me "a letter to our family community" that he had just written and distributed. He reported that "At the beginning of the last year, the Boston School Department called all of its principals together for a three-day professional development that began with them telling us that MCAS [Massachusetts Comprehensive Assessment System] is *everything* from now on. There was no dialogue, just an assumption that this was good and we were all to get on board."

Perrigo's letter, which follows, began his dialogue on the subject of standardized testing. I find this correspondence an impressive piece of work and an example of the power, insight, craft knowledge—and moral outrage—that can emerge when an experienced practitioner puts pen to paper. I am also impressed with the important issues he raises and how absent they are from the contemporary discourse on standardized tests and testing. How much our profession needs more of these notes from the field.

December 6, 1999

Dear parents and guardians of
New Mission High School students,

In a few days, the Department of Education will release the long-awaited scores on last spring's Massachusetts Comprehensive Assessment System (MCAS) test. There will continue to be a lot of media attention given to the controversy surrounding the MCAS.

At New Mission we have some serious concerns about the MCAS test and the state's plans to use it, and only it, to decide (1) if students receive high school diplomas and (2) if schools are doing a good job educating young people. I'd like our community to begin an important conversation about these concerns.

Is the MCAS *a "good" test?* There are many ways to describe the qualities of a good test, but in its simplest form a good test should reveal important information about our students. The state claims that the MCAS measures "essential knowledge," analytical skills important to that knowledge, and the ability to apply that knowledge to real-world situations. This sounds great, but a closer look at the test itself raises doubts about this claim. The amount of "knowledge" that the test requires is so vast as to seem ludicrous. Is it important, for example, that every tenth grader in the state know the effect of Confucian philosophy on the civil service entrance exam in the Ming Dynasty in fourteenth-century China? Who decides this? I will confess, I don't think I could pass the MCAS, and I think many other relatively "successful" adults would have trouble as well! Should this concern us?

Though the test has several "open response" sections designed to test thinking processes, most of the test still relies on the old-fashioned multiple-choice format. These tests are mostly testing memory. The definition of an educated person in the twenty-first century is not a person who can reproduce lots of unconnected facts that have been stuffed into his or her brain. Students who do well on these tests might have great careers as *Jeopardy* contestants on TV, but they are being cheated out of a meaningful education. At New Mission we value conceptual thinking, initiative, reflection, creativity, imagination, originality, effort, curiosity, collaboration, communication, and a host of other things we all think are important. Does the MCAS test any of this?

Is MCAS *going to have an impact on the quality of education our students receive?* There is good reason to believe that the emphasis put on standardized tests makes the education of our young people worse, not better. Under pressure to raise test scores, good teachers across the state are abandoning important teaching and beginning to teach to the test. Valuable class time is being spent on drills, test-taking techniques, practice tests, and rushing superficially through huge amounts of material that students may not remember even until they take the MCAS. Schools are slowly being turned into giant test prep centers. Many important things that can't be so easily quantified get sacrificed: time to consider important ideas, to explore complex issues, to experiment and question, to discuss in depth with others, and many of the other practices that we know make for meaningful learning. MCAS puts a high value on the least significant aspects of learning. It's too high a price!

Can we trust the MCAS *results?* No one test should ever be used by itself to make important educational decisions. The analysis of the MCAS results are laid out using a lot of complicated numbers, fancy charts, and multicolored graphs. It appears very professional and scientific, but let's not forget where all these fancy numbers come from. They come from real kids, our kids, sitting at desks for hours and hours trying to figure out why they should care about this grueling but seemingly meaningless task. (The test takes about eighteen hours to complete!) I was in the room with them. I know what they were going through, hour after hour, day after day. I wanted, in the worst way, for them to do well on it, in spite of the reservations I have about this test. I did my best to convince them to try their hardest. But the test will not be used to determine graduation (or anything else) until 2003, so, really, why should they care?

I observed in our students three basic responses to the test: Students who took it very seriously and whose anxiety level about it was often very high; students who tried initially, but eventually ran out of steam and gave up; and students who blew off most of the test from the beginning. In all three of these cases, we have to question how seriously we should take the scores.

We also know that sometimes very talented students do poorly on these tests, whereas not-so-good students sometimes do well.

There are many reasons for this. It is possible, for example, for a student to remember a set of rules that will lead to selecting a right answer on a test, but the student may not have clear understanding of the concepts involved. Conversely, a good grasp of the concept, but a minor error in calculation could result in a wrong answer. In both cases, the test would inadequately classify the student.

Do we need to be particularly concerned about our students? A recent study by the Gaston Institute at UMass predicts that if the test were given today, huge percentages of Black and Latino students would fail the test and therefore be denied a diploma. Expectations are that dropout rates for these students will rise dramatically. Evidence suggests that white students from working-class families may not fare much better. We know too well the implications of this, and it has to raise serious concerns about the direction in which our society is moving.

At New Mission, we use a variety of methods to determine how well our students are doing. There is no doubt that many of our students need serious improvement. For exactly this reason, our students will be hurt the most by MCAS. And remember, we can't fatten the cow by weighing it!

If a school's test scores go up, does it mean that the school is doing a good job? The state is comparing a school's test scores over three years to monitor for improvement. But each year, it is a completely different group of students being tested. So how does this show improvement? The state argues that over three years a trend can be identified. That defies basic logic.

In order to do well on tests, students are often taught tricks that are not necessarily good habits for learning. Skimming, looking at the answers before the question, skipping the hard parts, or guessing may lead one to do well on a test, but could lead to a more superficial attitude towards learning in general. Schools' test scores going up is an indication that they have learned to "take the tests" better, not necessarily that education has improved.

Is the MCAS *here to stay?* The law that created MCAS never intended for the assessment used to grant high school diplomas to be a single standardized test. The MCAS was created in a very charged political climate that demanded more accountability from schools. This does not mean that it is educationally sound. There are ways to hold schools accountable without destroying them. What is done politically can be undone politically.

I have a great interest in living in a more just and equitable world. To that end, much of my life has been invested in the development of young people. I have believed for a long time that better schools lead to a better world. But I have to tell you, I'm not sleeping very well at night these days.

I am very honored that you have entrusted the education of your sons and daughters to New Mission, but I don't want you to take my word alone for any of this. I suggest we dedicate our January Family Council meeting to looking closely at some of the test and discussing what we see. Then we can put our ideas together and figure out where to go.

Sincerely,

David R. Perrigo
Director
New Mission High School
Boston Public Schools

APPENDIX B: SOME THOUGHTS ON "CONDITIONS FOR LEARNING"

Barbara Soisson, curriculum coordinator at Lake Oswego Junior High School in Lake Oswego, Oregon, wrote the paper that follows. She was assisted by Fred Locke Jr., magnet coordinator for performing and visual arts at Jefferson High School in Portland, Oregon, and by Anita Gaskill, principal at East Orient Elementary School in Gresham, Oregon.

Barbara Soisson commented on how these three colleagues collaborated to create the final product, which was presented as part of their graduate study at Lewis and Clark College. Inspired by the seventeen conditions for learning (outlined in Chapter Twelve), "we used the metaphor of the dance as a work in progress. A dance is the performance, what we want to achieve. Fred taught a group of aspiring administrators some simple steps to a complex dance routine. We practiced, put it all together, then watched his students' polished performance. I looked at some of the everyday practices in schools and wrote about ways to work toward approaching what we want to achieve as learners. Anita articulated the importance of educators' viewing themselves as learners and recognizing the steps and ongoing efforts involved in creating a better school."

This appendix has been adapted from the original.

Recognition

Sometimes the recognition given to learners seems superficial, as do the extrinsic rewards given to students. If learning is to be valued and taken seriously, it is important to do more than give folks a hand at a staff meeting. Sincere updates about what staff members are working on, in verbal form and in written communication, can set a different tone. At staff meetings, principals can ask staff members to talk briefly, either in groups or individually, about their work and learning. Meeting agendas should always have room left to allow staff members to positively share experiences; this would also contribute to a flexible and spontaneous atmosphere. School newsletters can note learners' efforts. There could be a bulletin board in the main hallway that showcases what members of the school community are contributing to the school. Administrators could also approach staff members and let them know that they are doing valuable work, invite individuals to participate in a staff reading group, and show interest in their findings. An authentic way to show staff members that their work and ideas are valued would be to ask for a wish list from each department chair or team leader at the beginning of the school year and to use it in planning and budgeting. An additional list could be asked for halfway through the school year. Making these lists would actually involve the whole staff, because department chairs or team leaders would first need to collaborate and prioritize in order to come up with list items.

Learner-Centered

The school leader or principal could periodically poll staff members to find out what they would like to explore during in-services, discuss at staff meetings, and suggest as possible topics for focus groups. A large chart could be kept in the staff room for ideas. Administrators would then build time for these individual teaching and curriculum interests into the in-service schedule, balancing them with mandated building and district topics; in some cases, administrators could offer a menu. Staff members need to be questioned about what they want to explore, both individually and as a group, in order to initiate schoolwide conversation about learning. Principals who share their own stories about their work and learning will introduce an atmosphere and attitude that is more conducive to learning for everyone and make this more than another staff development exercise. Teacher leaders or principals can help individuals examine their background interests, teaching passions, and concerns to identify possible areas of learning simply by talking about them.

A Culture of Playfulness

On a large scale, an atmosphere of playfulness comes from the dance, the sailing experience, or the special staff activity that encourages everyone to set aside daily work concerns and just enjoy learning. Teacher leaders or principals could log some of the participants' creative actions and comments in order to make connections between this experience and our daily work and learning. They can debrief the activities and structure discussions that let participants see applications for the activities and behaviors that occurred in a playful setting.

Playfulness also means infusing celebration and fun into our regular teaching lives. Beginning or ending meetings with brief discussions of what we've learned recently from our students and colleagues could result in spontaneous and humorous responses. Staff will more readily buy into learning if leaders support play, and model that it's OK to be playful and creative because leaders truly believe that staff all know how to get back to work. Modeling is done when principals and leaders provide opportunities for play and give individuals positive feedback about their creative contributions. It is the role of the teacher leader or principal to plan discussions or provide the written and verbal comments that connect playful learning to our ongoing learning as educators. The more creative and fun learning becomes for all teachers, administrators, and students, the more valuable it will be, especially because the adults should be modeling what they want to see the students doing. Fun is engaging, and engaged learners can be very productive when their efforts are guided. Such guidance is necessary, especially to help skeptical staff see creative activities as more than feel-good exercises that waste time.

Risk-Taking

We all know that it's good, and often necessary, to take risks in order to grow personally and professionally. Still, the demands and structure of the organization discourage risk-taking. Leaders could encourage risk-taking by modeling it—for example, by telling staff about a professional risk that they are currently taking, then describing the saga. Updating staff, continuing the story—either verbally when addressing the large group or in those weekly school memos—is a way to acknowledge that risk-taking has peaks and pitfalls. (It might also enliven those deadly memos.) Leaders also need to initiate and guide staff through a risk-taking move: identifying the nature of the risk, providing opportunities to discuss problems and progress, but most of all letting staff members see themselves as risk-takers. It's important to involve participants in shaping the risk as much as possible. The cooperative shaping of risks so that all those involved feel responsible and excited about the possible outcomes is part of a learning atmosphere. A complete schedule change or the formation of interdisciplinary teams could be seen as nothing more than an imposed change rather than a risk that's being taken to improve conditions for kids, unless leaders provide staff with opportunities to take such mandates and lace them with their own ideas.

Visibility as a Learner

To help ensure that the visibility that results from people identifying themselves as learners is not setting them up for risk-taking that makes them feel merely vulnerable, leaders need to take steps that allow staff to take ownership of the learning. Accountability is still somewhat removed from the school and its staff. Test results may be published in the newspapers, but decisions are made at the state and district level. If leaders persistently ask staff members how they plan to share and use what they learn, some control is returned to the school and its teachers. This discussion can take place individually as staff members identify what they want to explore, and as a group when the staff plans how to measure the progress that is being made. The "how" part of the discussion is as vital to improvement as the actual results, because it requires teachers to talk about methods and about what is meaningful in terms of outcomes. In addition, the "how" process is valuable because it promotes collaboration between teachers and administrators, who can then learn from each other. Leaders need to talk about measurement and accountability as tools for those who are participating in learning, tools that give educators a means of making sure their valuable time is well spent.

That You Are Learning, What You Are Learning

Again, the emphasis for leaders must be on engaging everyone in learning, on involving everyone in the process. This involvement encourages creativity, an essential ingredient of good engaged learning and problem solving. Giving staff members the freedom to select topics and areas of interest can minimize resistance to trying yet another theory. To really make this happen, leaders need to set aside time to "make the rounds" and converse with individuals. This supplements the routine of looking into classrooms, which sometimes gives teachers the impression that someone is just checking up on them. By soliciting teachers' thoughts and views, leaders treat teachers as more than keepers of the classrooms; they are part of a professional organization. Leaders, in this case principals, could also ask teachers to base one of their yearly professional goals on their own learning interests. It would be self-evaluated and discussed with the principal. Because much of the evaluation process is merely a mandated procedure, this could give teachers and principals another opportunity to converse about what they are learning from each other.

Constructing One's Own Knowledge

Leaders, of course, should both shape and use the knowledge they acquire. And they should allow those around them to see what their leaders are learning. Finally, leaders need to expect faculty members to structure opportunities for themselves, to create *their* own knowledge. They could do this by facilitating work sessions in which teachers synthesize theory and make specific applications for their own schools, disciplines, grade levels, and classrooms. Teachers need time to assimilate and practice using new materials and approaches so that they can model them with confidence and success. Then time must be allocated for teachers to evaluate these applications. This approach could also help move schools away from the model whereby teachers are shown what to do, allowed to discuss it during the workshop, then expected to just put it into practice.

Incorporating the Liberal Arts

Leaders can use the liberal arts as a context for discussion of the day-to-day efforts and changes we are making in education. First, they can draw examples from history, literature, and the arts to illustrate the evolving thinking that leads to change within disciplines. (It almost goes without saying that change isn't always regarded positively within a school.) Historians, for example, have long debated the merits of integrating the study of sociology, geography, anthropology, and economics with the study of history. This serves as a rationale for interdisciplinary studies. In turn, it fosters learning from each other by allowing students to gain a complete understanding and appreciation for a particular group of people. From literature we know that many first novels are at least partially autobiographical. Writers learn to write about what they truly know, and separating the writer from the work isn't possible or desirable. As schools weigh the amount of emphasis to give both the child and the subject matter, this example can be elaborated on to discuss what is developmentally appropriate at different levels.

Second, integrating education and the liberal arts gives those of us who work in schools a more balanced perspective if we can remind ourselves that education is an art, especially considering that so many comparisons attempt to equate schools with businesses. By validating the artistic component of education, we are recognizing the beauty and importance of human interaction and creativity. Logistically much of education needs to be businesslike, but we can also build a framework for the truly stimulating and engaging side of learning.

Inventive Irreverence

If leaders want to promote learning and be seen as learners, it is necessary to sidestep the marching orders occasionally so that staff can see how leaders view actions and decisions. Sharing personal educational beliefs during discussions about policy and implementation can reveal one's human side and inspire others to recall their own principles.

A Sense of Wonder

The imposed order in schools promotes quick reactions from students and staff. We respond to the yoke of routine. One way to nurture some sense of wonder would be to invite questions as part of tending to daily business. The principal or leader is not someone who answers all questions but can be the one who calls for them, organizes them into topics for discussion, and identifies common themes the staff may wish to examine. Effective teachers ask, "What are your questions?" before moving on to new information. Teacher leaders and principals could make questions the top item on meeting agendas, not the item left in case there is time at the end. The regular sharing of best practices lets colleagues inspire each other and invites interdisciplinary collaboration. It is also important to suggest ways for staff members to note their own observations. Eliminating or trading off one paperwork task in exchange for making daily observations in a teaching log would give people a chance to begin looking at their work and forming questions, even if for a limited period of time.

High Expectations

Teacher leaders and principals can model their own high expectations by stating some individual professional goals. Ultimately, staff members need to articulate their own expectations for the school and for themselves. Therefore, initially trusting that individuals will gravitate toward higher expectations if they own those expectations and examine the results of goals set from those expectations can encourage people to participate in the process of setting high expectations; they don't have to be told that the school or the principal has them. Setting expectations and assessing progress are staff exercises that should be in place at all levels. Individuals can set personal goals, departments or teams can set goals, and the school staff can set goals. Similarly, the student body, grade levels, and classes can set goals. Looking for commonalities among all these goals helps create a sense of community. Also, principals should ask teachers to talk about their expectations for themselves and their students during annual goal-setting conferences, then refer back to them throughout the year. Teacher leaders should include everyone's expectations about what a team or curriculum group is to accomplish, and use this information to set meeting agendas. Staff should evaluate administrators, using the goals that have been stated. Engaging in periodic discussions about "where we are," celebrating progress, and clarifying expectations are essential to keep talk of high expectations from becoming merely more talk.

Collegiality

It seems that teachers and administrators within a school often put more energy into finding ways to maintain working relationships by adding social activities than by looking for ways that everyone

Variety

One way for a leader to view this condition for learning is to recognize that not all of these learning conditions will bring results for and from everyone but that by offering multiple activities and opportunities, there is a rung for everyone to grab.

• • •

Teachers need to see administrators who model themselves as learners; but in order to replenish themselves, administrators need role models also. There does not have to be a top-down approach here. Principals who are open to learning from teachers, and who acknowledge that learning, will enhance the learning atmosphere in the school. Forming fluid small groups around interests and current concerns can support individual learning. Sharing groups' findings with the rest of the staff is a way to further a commitment to learning; doing so makes people aware of what others are learning and how they are working with what they have learned. The whole school as a community of learners should be ultimately engaged in learning from and with each other.

NOTES

Introduction

1. *Education Week*, Apr. 30, 1997, p. 37.

Chapter Two

1. J. Saphier and M. King, "Good Seeds Grow in Strong Cultures," *Educational Leadership*, Mar. 1985, pp. 67–74.
2. T. H. White, *The Sword in the Stone*. New York: Philomel Books, 1993, p. 228.
3. For a further discussion of the limitations of the conventional forms of teacher evaluation by the principal, and for a better, if more demanding, way, one which can promote both learning and community, see K. Marshall, "How I Confronted HSPS (Hyperactive Superficial Principal Syndrome) and Began to Deal with the Heart of the Matter," *Phi Delta Kappan*, Jan. 1996, pp. 336–345.

Chapter Four

1. "The Report Card on the Ethics of American Youth," compiled by the Josephson Institute of Ethics, as reported in *USA Today*, Oct. 16, 2000.
2. Here are the questions I posed: What significant risks have you taken during your period of study here? What legacy of lasting value are you leaving behind, here within this school community? When you look back in a decade on your years

of study here, what do you predict you will find were the most lasting, most profound learnings you experienced—and retained? How would you characterize yourself, after this college experience, as a lifelong learner?

3. G. Michie, *Holler If You Hear Me*. New York: Teachers College Press, 1999.
4. *USA Today*, Oct. 17, 2000, p. 6D.

Chapter Five

1. All of the anecdotes from MicroSociety schools come from personal correspondence with George Richmond, president of MicroSociety, Inc.
2. Research by J. Hattie et al., as reported in *Education Week*, May 7, 1997, p. 8.

Chapter Six

1. Research conducted at Dartmouth Medical School, as reported by G. T. O'Connor in the *Journal of the American Medical Association*, March 1996.
2. Alumni Advanced Symposium for Principals, Association of California School Administrators, July 1999.
3. I found an excellent example of a thoughtful challenge to policymakers when I visited New Mission High School, a pilot school within the Boston public schools. David R. Perrigo, the director of the school, has much to say to parents (and others) about the high-stakes testing in Massachusetts (see Appendix A).

Chapter Seven

1. J. Brown and D. Issacs, "Conversation as a Core Business Process," *Systems Thinker*, Dec.-Jan. 1996–1997.

Chapter Eight

1. *Education Week*, Feb. 24, 1999, p. 15.

Chapter Nine

1. These are the words of Susan Naysnerski. All the cited quotations in this chapter are from Rhode Island teachers.
2. Ron Poirier.
3. Judy Hede McGowan.
4. Ruth Jernigan.
5. Ron Poirier.
6. Diane Kern.
7. Wendy Lombardi.
8. Sharon Webster.
9. Ruth Jernigan.
10. Vin Doyle.
11. Judy Hede McGowan.
12. Wendy Lombardi.
13. Unidentified Rhode Island teacher.
14. Unidentified Rhode Island teacher.
15. Wendy Lombardi.
16. Diane Kern.
17. Sharon Webster.
18. Ruth Jernigan.
19. Wendy Lombardi.
20. Patrick Kelly.
21. Diane Kern.
22. Vin Doyle.
23. Unidentified Rhode Island teacher.
24. Nancy Carnevale.
25. Unidentified Rhode Island teacher.
26. Helen Johnson.
27. Lisa Zavota.

28. Michael Neubauer.
29. Ron Poirier.
30. Judy Hede McGowan.

Chapter Ten

1. Lisa Zavota.
2. Denise Frederick.
3. Nancy Carnevale.
4. Ruth Jernigan.
5. Ruth Jernigan.
6. Unidentified Rhode Island teacher.
7. Susan Naysnerski.
8. Denise Frederick.
9. Deborah Meier, personal conversation.
10. Michael Neubauer.

Chapter Eleven

1. B. O. Brent, "Teaching in Educational Administration," *Newsletter of the American Educational Research Association*, Oct. 1998, 5(2).
2. Amy elaborates, "PMU stands for Pick Me Up. This is how we start every day at the MET. It is a morning meeting involving the whole school, during which time someone from the school community or an outside guest shares a talent or skill to inspire the students. Students or staff do anything from reading poems to playing an instrument, doing a scene from a play, talking about an internship, or describing a trip taken."
3. The Aspiring Principals' Program (175 Westminster Street, Providence, RI 02903), 1999.
4. The Aspiring Principals' Program currently has centers in Providence and Boston. For more information about the program, contact The Big Picture Company, 275B Westminster Street, Suite 500, Providence, RI 02903.

Chapter Twelve

1. The International Network of Principals' Centers, Harvard Graduate School of Education, 336 Gutman Library, Cambridge, MA 02138, (617) 495-9812.
2. The Principals' Center for the Garden State is located at 195 Nassau Street, Suite 12, Princeton, NJ 08542.
3. These are the words of Joanne Kerekes, a Dodge Fellow. The quotations that follow came from the written or spoken words of members of the first five cohorts of the Dodge Foundation program.
4. Claudia Radeke.
5. Elaine Pace.
6. Francesca Plain.
7. Ralph Ferrie.
8. Lillian Augustine.
9. Lillian Augustine.
10. Harlene Galen.
11. Meryl Barrett.
12. Nancy Richmond.
13. Unidentified Dodge Fellow.
14. Myra Lustberg.
15. Myra Lustberg.
16. William Sheridan.
17. Lillian Augustine.
18. Margaret Hayes.
19. Bruce Segall.
20. Delores Foster.
21. Lorraine Brooks.
22. Michael Gorman.
23. Debra Pavignano.
24. Lillian Augustine.
25. Myra Lustberg.
26. Unidentified Dodge Fellow.
27. Debra Pavignano.

28. Meryl Barrett.
29. Debra Pavignano.
30. Meryl Barrett.
31. Unidentified Dodge Fellow.
32. Ernest Palestis.
33. Harlene Galen.
34. Meryl Barrett.
35. Barbara Soisson, Fred Locke Jr., and Anita Gaskill collaborated to produce a document about how these conditions might be introduced into the culture of schools. See Appendix B.

Chapter Fourteen

1. T. E. Lawrence, *The Seven Pillars of Wisdom*. New York: Penguin, 1962.

Chapter Fifteen

1. D. Hagstrom, excerpted from his manuscript, "Honor the People, It's the Leaders Work: Stories That Make Our Heart Sing."

INDEX

U

V

W

Grateful acknowledgment is made for permission to quote from the following works:

The Sword in the Stone, by T. H. White. Copyright © 1993 Philomel Books, New York, NY. Used by permission of David Higham Associates.

Some of the chapters in *Learning by Heart* contain, in modified form, material by Roland S. Barth that has been previously published elsewhere, as follows:

"School and University: Bad Dreams, Good Dreams," *On Common Ground*, Number 6, Spring 1996. Portions of this article have been adapted and included in Chapter Three, with permission from the Yale-New Haven Teachers Institute, New Haven, CT.

"Building a Community of Learners," *Principal*, March 2000, Alexandria, Virginia. Portions of this article have been adapted and included, with permission, in Chapter Three.

"From Puddle Dock to the Twenty-First Century," in Rebecca van der Bogert (editor), *Making Learning Communities Work: The Critical Role of Leader as Learner*. New Directions for School Leadership, no. 7. San Francisco: Jossey-Bass, Spring 1998. Portions of this chapter have been adapted and included in Chapters Four, Five, and Eleven and in the Epilogue, with permission of John Wiley & Sons.

The Teacher Leader. Copyright © 1999 The Rhode Island Foundation, One Union Station, Providence, RI 02903. Portions have been adapted and included in Chapters Eight, Nine, and Ten, with permission of The Rhode Island Foundation.

Improving Schools from Within. Copyright © 1990 by Jossey-Bass. Portions of this book have been adapted and included in Chapters Ten and Fourteen, with permission of John Wiley & Sons.

"The Leader as Learner: Then and Now," *Alumni Bulletin*, December 1995. Portions of this article have been adapted and included in Chapter Twelve, with permission of the Harvard Graduate School of Education, Cambridge, MA.

The Principal Learner: A Work in Progress. Copyright © 1996 by the Geraldine R. Dodge Foundation, Morristown, NJ. Published by and available from the International Network of Principals' Centers, Harvard Graduate School of Education, Cambridge, MA 02138. Portions of this work have been adapted and included in Chapter Twelve, with permission of the Geraldine R. Dodge Foundation.

"Restructuring Schools: Some Questions for Teachers and Principals," *Phi Delta Kappan*, October 1991. Portions of this article have been adapted and included in Chapter Thirteen, with permission of Phi Delta Kappa International.

"Coming to a Vision," *Journal of Staff Development*, Volume 14, Number 1, Winter 1993. Portions of this article have been adapted and included in Chapter Fifteen, with permission of the National Staff Development Council, 2000.